Witchcraft: A Very Short Introduction

VERY SHORT INTRODUCTIONS are for anyone wanting a stimulating and accessible way in to a new subject. They are written by experts, and have been published in more than 25 languages worldwide.

The series began in 1995, and now represents a wide variety of topics in history, philosophy, religion, science, and the humanities. The VSI library now contains over 200 volumes—a Very Short Introduction to everything from ancient Egypt and Indian philosophy to conceptual art and cosmology—and will continue to grow to a library of around 300 titles.

Very Short Introductions available now:

For more information visit our web site
www.oup.co.uk/general/vsi/

Malcolm Gaskill

WITCHCRAFT

A Very Short Introduction

OXFORD
UNIVERSITY PRESS

OXFORD
UNIVERSITY PRESS

Great Clarendon Street, Oxford OX2 6DP

Oxford University Press is a department of the University of Oxford.
It furthers the University's objective of excellence in research, scholarship,
and education by publishing worldwide in

Oxford New York

Auckland Cape Town Dar es Salaam Hong Kong Karachi
Kuala Lumpur Madrid Melbourne Mexico City Nairobi
New Delhi Shanghai Taipei Toronto

With offices in

Argentina Austria Brazil Chile Czech Republic France Greece
Guatemala Hungary Italy Japan Poland Portugal Singapore
South Korea Switzerland Thailand Turkey Ukraine Vietnam

Oxford is a registered trade mark of Oxford University Press
in the UK and in certain other countries

Published in the United States
by Oxford University Press Inc., New York

© Malcolm Gaskill 2010

The moral rights of the author have been asserted
Database right Oxford University Press (maker)

First published 2010

British Library Cataloguing in Publication Data
Data available

Library of Congress Cataloging in Publication Data
Data available

Typeset by SPI Publisher Services, Pondicherry, India
Printed in Great Britain by
Ashford Colour Press Ltd, Gosport, Hampshire

ISBN 978-0-19-923695-4

Impression: 13

For Caroline and Geoffrey Roughton

Contents

Preface

When the historian Lucien Febvre said that 'a book on witches is a book which will be read' he wasn't trying to cajole a publisher, although I have myself used his words this way. I hope he's right. It's certainly a subject that has interested my family, friends, and students over the last two decades – unless they've all been spectacularly polite. The point of studying witchcraft can be hard to explain beyond the superficial allure of the mysterious and macabre. An old college friend, now a Privy Councillor, is as amused and baffled as ever that I'm still marking sites of witch-accusations on maps with a red pen.

So that is my purpose: to put succinctly into writing everything that I've struggled to convey verbally. Witchcraft is an undeniably strange subject, at once familiar and arcane, and insidious too. It just won't leave me alone, however hard I try to move on; colleagues have found the same. With any luck I can gather my thoughts here, drawing a line under my investigation into witches – until next time, of course.

For a solitary occupation, writing involves a lot of people. I want to thank Luciana O'Flaherty who commissioned the book, and Ronald Hutton who put her up to it. Ronald kindly commented on a complete draft, as did Stuart Clark, Brian Levack, and Willem de Blécourt. My editors, Andrea Keegan and Emma Marchant, were patient and encouraging; I am also indebted to Erica Martin for sorting out the illustrations, to Alyson Silverwood for some first-rate copy-editing, and to Kay Clement for diligently checking the proofs. Twenty years ago Keith Wrightson taught me how to be a historian, a debt impossible to repay. Recently Andy Wood and John Charmley, colleagues at the University of East Anglia, have treated me to much good humour and kindness. My parents Audrey and Eddie Gaskill have always been caring and intelligent participants in my work. Special thanks go to Sheena Peirse for putting up with me – my presence as well as my absence. Looking back over many years, I'd like to acknowledge another contribution without which I might never have got started. This was made by Caroline and Geoffrey Roughton, exemplars of generosity and pragmatism; it is to them that I dedicate this book with love and gratitude.

List of illustrations

Chapter 1
Fear

The idea of witchcraft

What is witchcraft? Here's what my dictionary says: 'the practices of a witch or witches, especially the use of magic or sorcery; the exercise of supernatural power supposed to be possessed by a person in league with the devil or evil spirits'. That's fine, unless you're the curious type. What do we mean by magic and sorcery? How does one access this supernatural power? Just who are the witches? These questions are difficult and generate questions of their own, expanding the problem, blurring definitions.

People prefer clear-cut definitions to blurred ones, order to chaos. We want existence to be comprehensible and governable, and so habitually classify it using simple 'binary oppositions': night and day, life and death, good and evil, human and beast. These extremes, positively and negatively charged, mark out a mental grid for arranging and interpreting thought and perception. Seen this way, the term 'witch' implies someone not like us, the opposite of an ideal. Witches are monsters haunting our dreams, confirming who we are through what we are not.

Except witches are *human*. Unlike monsters, they belong to society – a disguised enemy within. They are 'other', and yet they are also 'us'. Witches are living projections of feelings that defy easy rationalization or reconciliation: amity and enmity, compassion and cruelty, self-confidence and fear. Here we discover a basic human characteristic. For all our aspirations to reason, we are driven to act by emotion as much as by logic (of which more in a moment). Witches embody emotional ambiguity, straddling boundaries between life and death, night and day – subconscious manifestations of complex, often conflicted, relationships. Witchcraft is hard to define because it involves aspects of ourselves as a species, and as individuals, that trouble us.

We find witchcraft today and in antiquity, in the developing world and in rich nations; it's familiar to young and old, high and low. Some label enemies 'witches', while others profess or confess witches' skills. There are those who believe, and those who do not (especially in the West); but everyone recognizes the witch-figure. At the same time, the picture is always clouded, with no blue skies of truth beyond. This is the reality of witchcraft; we must accept it in all its murkiness. Witchcraft is a human occupation, but it isn't like carpentry or banking because it engages with an unseen world. It's hard to think, talk, and write about witches because they are essentially mysterious, occult – a word meaning 'hidden'. Marina Warner nails the problem:

> the supernatural is difficult terrain; of its very nature, it resists discourse; or, to put it more accurately, it is always in the process of being described, conjured, made, and made up, without ascertainable outside referents.

Witchcraft hovers, invisible yet powerful and persistent.

I teach history in a university, where I run a course on witchcraft in early modern Europe – between 1450 and 1750, when the idea of witchcraft was put frighteningly into practice. I've been studying the subject for twenty years, and have written four books including this one. I've learned that witches resist simplification, and are as diverse and complicated as the contexts to which they belong: economy, politics, religion, family, community, and mentality. Sometimes I get a funny look when I tell people about my speciality, as if I were a priest to a satanic coven. I'm not: I'm a historian, and for me witchcraft offers a glimpse into the intimate spaces and intricate mechanisms of past lives. Anthropologists studying tribal societies are interested in witches for the same reason. They have a word for the no-man's land between binary oppositions: the *liminal* – a grey area inhabited by things (and people) that don't fit obvious categories.

I became properly interested in witchcraft while a student, but, like most, had acquired some knowledge in childhood. Witches wore pointed hats and flew on broomsticks with cats perched on the end. They lived alone in tumble-down cottages, their warty faces illuminated by fires beneath bubbling cauldrons. This was an image reinforced at Halloween: the witch as monster, as 'other', as scapegoat. But there was always a puzzling ambiguity – or liminality – to witchcraft. One Christmas I was given a board-game called 'Haunted House', in which cardboard walls slotted into a base and players moved from room to room, menaced by witches. One was called 'Ghoulish Gertie', who dropped a whammy ball down the chimney; another 'Wanda the Wicked', she turned you into a mouse. But there was a third witch called 'Glenda the Good' who reversed Wanda's spells. If witches could be good as well as bad, what made them witches?

This paradox is important. Objective definitions of 'witchcraft' are unsatisfactory because its real meaning derives from relationships, shared experiences, and individual feelings. It is subjectively constituted, and consequently witches are far from homogenous in type. Back to the dictionary for an illustration. Under 'witch', we find 'an ugly, repulsive, or malevolent (usually old) woman; a hag' – in other words, 'Ghoulish Gertie'. But an alternative definition follows: 'a fascinating bewitching girl or young woman'. Which is it

3

1. Stereotypical old witch flying over the sea. Note the obligatory pointed hat, black cat, and broomstick

to be: repulsive or fascinating, young or old? Perhaps all these things. And therein lies the variety and ambiguity that we need to capture.

Meanings of witchcraft are so varied because the concept is so versatile. Wicca is a recognized religion whose adherents call themselves 'witches'. Children's fiction, horror films, and newspaper cartoons all make use of witches, drawing on shared ideas and imagery. 'Witch-hunt' commonly describes even modest antagonisms and injustices, and 'witch' remains an insult directed at women. Witchcraft is culturally durable, relevant, and potent – hard-wired into us all, even those who have consigned it to history's dustbin with other relics of primitivism. Witches are special. Cathars, Lollards, and Quakers were all persecuted, but it's hard to imagine a board-game about them. Why? Because they existed solidly and exclusively in the natural world, without much mystery. Witches, however, bother the subconscious. This is why we like them, hate them, can't do without them. This is why, in mint condition, a 'Haunted House' set from the early 1970s (US title: 'Which Witch?') changes hands for the price of a decent dinner for two. For collectors, this game is more than a key to nostalgia: it reconnects them with an intoxicating fantasy picked up in childhood and never completely shaken off.

This is a book about witchcraft as a human phenomenon, past and present. One of its aims is to involve you, the reader, in the story of the witch over time. I want to bring witchcraft closer to *your* fears and fantasies rather than distancing it from the comforts and certainties of modern life. The historian of witchcraft Robin Briggs suggests that 'just as rabbits have a "hawk detector" in their retina, so human beings have a "witch detector" somewhere in their consciousness, and derive excitement from having it activated'. If this is true, witchcraft involves nature as well as nurture, and to understand it we need to travel not just through history, but back into pre-history.

Ancient wisdom

You belong to the species *Homo sapiens* – a relative newcomer on earth. The planet is nearly 4,600 million years old, and, life-wise, for the first billion years not much happened. Then monocellular organisms ruled the world for 3 billion years before a multicellular version emerged. Only in the last 500 million years were they joined by aquatic animals. The dinosaurs came and went, after which, 65 million years ago, mammals and birds began to diversify, and for well over 64 million years there were no people to bother them. Clever humans, our ape-forebears' final model, entered the scene just 120,000 to 200,000 years ago – in roughly the last 1/30,000 of the terrestrial timeline.

Compared to other creatures, these humans were staggeringly advanced. Large brains encouraged complex cognition and language, and an upright stance and gait left hands free for tool-making. Flints cut flesh and friction made fire; hunting and gathering became organized. Behind these qualities lay consciousness. This state puzzles philosophers and biologists alike, yet it's fundamental to us all. As late as 1700, people may have lacked a modern sense of the self, but we share with our primordial ancestors a degree of introspection absent in moths, mice, and mammoths. Awareness of time is critical: day and night, lunar months, the seasons, the annual cycle, a lifespan. Like us, early humans knew fear, not just a defensive reflex but uncertainty and anxiety about the future. They contemplated their own mortality, a thought unknown in animals but which in humans has prompted millennia of odd behaviour.

Humans evolved to be emotional. Despite the negative view of thinkers from the Stoics to Spinoza, emotions help us break habits limiting our development; they encourage impulsiveness, often disastrous for the individual but beneficial to the group. And we are actually very good at manipulating our own emotions. Every time you cry in the cinema or cheer up in the pub, that's what you're doing. Rituals are crucial, whether individual and informal, or collective and formalized. Since the earliest times, prayer, sacrifice, feasting, funerary rites, and so on have substituted joy and hope for fear and despair. Planning helped early people survive bleak winters; but so did faith – galvanizing beliefs shaped and substantiated by social observance.

These developments were not deliberately contrived: cavemen did not ingeniously invent religion to perk themselves up. And psychological and emotional states took the forms they did because they were already infused with spiritual and mythological meaning. Emotion and religion, psychology and culture, were united in constitution and reciprocal in influence. But however spontaneous and unconscious the religious impulse was in its causes, the effect was that chaos felt controlled.

Hence a propensity for religion was an evolutionary advantage with an enduring legacy. We may be better than primitive man at postponing death, but we remain ignorant and afraid of what lies beyond. So religious sensibilities continue to thrive, especially in times of doubt and danger. Consciousness cannot meaningfully grasp its own extinction, and so it was perhaps inevitable that humans came to see themselves in terms of a body and a soul, the former transient and corruptible, the latter eternal and transcendent. We can't prove that cavemen appealed to spirits of the dead, but anthropological evidence would suggest that they did. This mystical tendency was not some passing phase of development, still less an error swept away by enlightened modernity. It was – and is – a defining characteristic of humanity.

In our quest for the origins of witchcraft, we shouldn't forget another human trait, one that resides uneasily with faith: restless curiosity. What's over that hill? Why are we dying of plague? How can I split this atom? Another expression of this is our yearning for origins, a need satisfied by myth. Creatures that had learned to make things in turn imagined the immanent makers of themselves and their world; God *may* have made man in his own image, but perhaps it was the other way round. Like spirits, most gods were invisible, necessitating rituals and stories – and the emotional states they induced – to effect communion and communication. This shouldn't be dismissed as folly. That the sun and the moon and the stars were deities, and that spirits could manifest in vapour or incarnate in men and beasts, were logical progressions of thought. Indeed, for most of human history, these were perfectly reasonable, workable assumptions. Contrary to our empirical habits of mind, belief and knowledge are inseparable.

There is one final ingredient. You may not feel homicidally competitive, but your genes tell a different story. Perhaps you live on a wage or pension or loan; perhaps you spent part of it on this book; I doubt you've ever been *really* hungry, still less that you'll ever starve. And yet the lives of most people who have ever lived have been dominated by the struggle to survive and reproduce, something for which evolution made careful preparation. Again, the emotions kick in. Hungry people are often angry, agitating as well as cooperating to secure resources. Society, however, cannot tolerate anarchy, so it has been the practice of civilizations to moderate hostility with law and custom. Among the unwritten rules of rural communities, one finds the principle of 'zero-sum gain': resources are finite, hence prosperity must have been achieved at another's expense. Unfair advantage, of course, can be gained through profiteering, extortion, trickery, and theft. But throughout history millions have believed, and in poorer parts of the globe believe still, in the supernatural pursuit of private ambition: harnessing intangible forces, commanding spirits, working magic – by any other name, witchcraft.

The rise of magic

Seeing witchcraft as a culturally embedded idea challenges the usual assumption that it was a category mistake, a surrender to emotion, a badge of ignorance. Not only did witch-beliefs make sense, and continue to make sense, but they delivered truths about the universe. Most of us don't examine closely what we know, partly because this would consume our time (and might lead to existential crisis), but also because we lack independent means of verification. Instead, we trust in the probable nature of things and outcomes; otherwise we would be paralysed. If air passengers insisted on conducting their own safety checks, no one would ever fly anywhere. Like knowledge, belief supports reality. *Homo erectus* walked tall and *Homo habilis* was dextrous; but *Homo sapiens* was the knowing human: conscious, cognitive, but credulous; a good thinker *and* a good believer – the key to evolutionary success.

However much history becomes equated with progress, all advances bring problems. Civilization, originating in Mesopotamia in the 6th millennium BC, was characterized by managed agriculture and sophisticated social organization. But for all the opportunity in this, settlement increased people's vulnerability to nature and one another. Droughts and blights ruined crops and livestock, floods and earthquakes levelled cities, fire and disease decimated populations, and the rootedness that comes from investment in things inhibited flight from the enemies those things attracted. Society, moreover, brought not just economic and commercial efficiency but hierarchy, subordination, and tension. Fear was promoted by civilization, likewise the antidote to fear: faith.

So far this book has dealt in speculative inferences, but civilization leaves the sort of documentary sources that reassure historians. We know a lot about ancient Mesopotamian religion, enough to see how closely it resembles all religions. There was a god of heaven and a consort whose name meant 'earth'; a sun god and a moon god; deities for every worry, from aches and pains to harvest failure. Knowledge was arranged oppositively and the cosmos swirled with intangible forces reacting to, and determining, human deeds – what we might call a 'morally reflexive universe'. There was a ghostly afterlife, although it wasn't much fun. At the heart of every community stood a temple, run by a priestly caste that conducted rituals and kept records. Spells and invocations were pressed into clay tablets. Less evidence exists for ordinary people, but we can assume that they feared for themselves and their families, and courted favour from gods and ancestral spirits. We know that they wished misfortune on their enemies because written injunctions against harmful magic survive.

The nuts and bolts of witchcraft therefore might be detected in the earliest civilization: the theism, animism, and conflict, as well as the legalism that defined cursing, the better to proscribe and punish it. Things were not much different in Egypt. Rituals, spells, and taboos were endemic, and the open frontier between this world and the next elaborately constructed. Greece and Rome followed the Egyptian lead. For all its grandeur and glory, the classical world was steeped in the dark manipulation of spirits; here was the means to alleviate anxiety, deploy anger, and satisfy desire. Nor was this residual or eccentric, a precursor to the arts and sciences later celebrated by an ascending West. Magic was part of an accepted and vibrant reality, integral to everyone's culture and mentality. When tracing our social ancestry back to the ancients, we should take the rough with the smooth – that is, the superstitious with the rational.

But how reliable are terms like 'superstitious' and 'rational'? This is a thorny problem: how to describe contemporary ideas faithfully using the idiom required by a modern audience. These two criteria are the 'emic' and the 'etic': the internal meaning of things in the past and their representation in the present. Unconsciously we draw lines between religion and magic, religion and science, science and superstition; but to our ancestors distinctions were less stark. To the Greeks and Romans – or even to most 17th-century Europeans – astronomy and astrology meant roughly the same thing. This chapter began with the difficulty of defining witchcraft, and the observation that dictionaries invoke concepts – 'magic', 'supernatural', 'evil' – that raise new questions. But the instability of the word 'witchcraft' consists not just in the passage of time – the etic slowly departing from the emic – but in perplexity, vagueness, and controversy at *the time* about what witchcraft might mean. An emic understanding of an idea may alienate us; but that doesn't mean the idea was simple or went unchallenged in its own age.

Names make our world and they beguile us. According to Wittgenstein, 'philosophy is a battle against the bewitchment (*Verhexung*) of our intelligence by means of language'. But history can help too. The philosopher also taught that the meaning of a word is determined by its use. And that's what this book is about: an exploration of the idea of witchcraft in different contexts over time. In all ages, rulers, theologians, and jurists, like modern lexicographers, have tried to pin witchcraft down; but its ontological status is volatile, the picture kaleidoscopic. In the most famous play about witchcraft, Macbeth greets the weird sisters

2. Mid-19th-century interpretation of Macbeth meeting the witches, who prophesy his future and so seal his fate

with a question: 'How now, you secret, black, and midnight hags!
What is't you do?' To which they reply: 'a deed without a name'.
Quite so. We depend on words, but they can get in the way.

Witchcraft reflects every facet of the human affairs that give rise to
it, its forms as capriciously varied as the minutiae of society and
politics, religion and culture. In ancient Greece, the term *mageia*
(the root of 'magic') became increasingly pejorative. Public demand
for magic exceeded what priests could supply, producing a plethora
of unofficial magicians. Since magic was unregulated power, these
men and women were seen to assume state authority and so fell
foul of the law. In Rome, too, the difference between healer and
hag was a matter of opinion, both individual and institutional: was
the witch the people's friend or a dangerous rebel? Despite
consensus that witchcraft was real, the more Romans thought
about it, the harder it became to say exactly what it was.

The taxonomy grew ever more complicated. By the later classical
period, witches were separated into the *saga*, or soothsayer; the
sortilega, or diviner by casting lots; the *venefica*, or spell-maker;
the *strix*, a vampiric night-flying owl; and the *lamia*, who like the
strix preyed on children – a timeless anxiety. But the
epistemological bedrock of these terms was uneven and flawed,
their proliferation and interchangeability a symptom of a
diversifying, dispersing, and ultimately ungovernable society.

Chapter 2
Heresy

Authority and orthodoxy

Worrying about witchcraft did not cause the decline of the Roman Empire, any more than it caused the Protestant Reformation, European wars of religion, English civil war, or the rise of African independence movements. And yet each of these events was accompanied by increased persecution of witches, a livid symptom of social and political turmoil. This is partly what makes witchcraft such a good peephole for historians and anthropologists. Far from being an end in itself, the study of witchcraft is a means to get at something else, something hidden or intangible. Some witchcraft scholars are interested in the state: not just polities and institutions, but dynamic relationships between households, communities, councils, and courts – micro and macro in urgent and endless reciprocity. From here they can survey the changing reality of power, and witchcraft is all about change and power.

The centrifugal pull of government maintains its integrity: the regulation of conduct upholds authority and keeps order. Religion has long been of utmost importance here; orthodoxy and loyalty go hand in hand. (Secular-minded readers in the UK take note: blasphemy was not fully decriminalized until July 2008, and the monarch remains 'defender of the faith'.) The Greeks and Romans condemned religious error, called *deisidaimonia* by the former and *superstitio* by the latter. Both cultures suppressed excessive fear of spirits and consequent devotion to unorthodox (e.g. Egyptian) gods and cults. The fact that the power of *daimones*, to use the Greek term, might be directed against personal enemies intensified official hostility. Such practices were not only antisocial: they usurped the right of the state to settle disputes and inflict punishment. This concern formed a template adapted and applied repeatedly in the Christian era, most famously in Europe between the 16th and 18th centuries amid intense political and legal centralization.

The advance of respectable magic – what we might call 'science' – accentuated the contrast between orthodox and unorthodox practices. At first, political and judicial authorities permitted sages to communicate with higher powers, while suppressing magical mayhem stirred up by vengeful plebs. But the distinction grew fainter, legal intolerance of magic more pronounced. According to the historian Livy, in the 2nd century BC some 5,000 Romans were executed for the crime of *veneficium*, the literal meaning of which – poisoning – had moved closer to *maleficium*: inflicting harm using magic. Then, in 33 BC, a nervous Senate banished all sorcerers and necromancers to protect public virtue and the viability of the state. Magic, specifically the *fear* of magic, raised vexing questions that remained unanswered in later periods. What was the relationship between magician and spirit? Was it some kind of pact, and, if so, did this constitute a false allegiance or, worse, heresy or treason? Should magic itself be punished, or only its destructive effects? How might one distinguish natural from preternatural phenomena? Were *daimones* good and bad, as Socrates had implied, or just bad – the opposite of gods?

Imperialism tests political strength. The periphery can threaten the centre, destabilizing national identity and undermining confidence. By encapsulating the 'other', witches help to ground vague fears and foster unity. Romans came to see witches as ruthless and lawless criminals, blaspheming, murdering, and messing with nature. Horace told of witches lurking in graveyards, offering libations to ghosts, and concocting a potion from a young boy's liver – horror stories that struck a chord in a nervous society (although the poet himself was sceptical). Colonization also brought Romans face to face with terrifying magic. Like English settlers shocked by 'devil-worshippers' in 17th-century America, legionaries on campaign swapped tales about their enemies' maleficent blood-rites. Tacitus describes the assault in AD 60 on the Isle of Anglesey, where British warriors and their witch-like women made a last stand. As the Romans crossed the water, they saw ranks of druids 'lifting up their hands to heaven, and pouring forth horrible imprecations'. Momentarily the troops froze but pushed on to lay waste the sacred groves where, it was alleged, human sacrifices were performed.

Ahead of Wittgenstein, the Victorian novelist Samuel Butler called words 'an attempt to grip or dissect that which in ultimate essence is as ungrippable as a shadow'. Witchcraft is particularly shadowy, maddeningly ungrippable. Its definitions are varied, its meanings relative. Our separation of religion and magic would have meant little to the ancients. Instead, they observed a distinction between, on the one hand, their own orthodox religion and magic, and distasteful foreign equivalents on the other. But the Roman definition was constantly changing, and by the late imperial period (3rd to 5th century AD), the threat posed by *superstitio* – fashionable but false religion – to civil society was fusing with the image of the nocturnal hag, and with the concept of *maleficium*, as reflected in a legal code of 297. The philosophers, priests, and legislators of the Christian era inherited these ideas, and were to complicate and muddle things up even more.

Thinking with demons

Samuel Butler also quipped that 'God as now generally conceived of is only the last witch'. But a similar thought had occurred to earlier generations. From the advent of Christianity in the West, it was suggested that Jesus was a skilled magician like Simon Magus, a charismatic Samaritan adept at levitation. It was the early Christian writers who forced the distinction: Christ was God incarnate; Simon at best a charlatan and wizard, at worst a demon or heretic. And so heresy became the label orthodox Christians attached to dangerous beliefs, although the absolute veracity of their own faith was easier to declare than demonstrate. The substance of debate was too metaphysical, too sublime, for that. Distinctions *had* to be forced, because they couldn't be proved.

This cut both ways. In AD 177, Christians at Lyons, self-styled warriors against Roman devilishness, were themselves accused of ritual black magic, incest, and cannibalism. Those who weren't lynched were thrown to wild animals, their remains burned. As we'll see later, the charge of witchcraft was never uniquely associated with one faith or another but generated by conflict *between* faiths. When, in the 4th century, Emperor Constantine converted and the Roman state gradually Christianized, the demonic threat shifted to Islam. Meanwhile within the empire newly adopted beliefs supported Manichaeism: the dualistic notion that God grappled with an equivalent Satan, a primeval battle between light and dark. For ordinary folk, therefore, there was a right way and a wrong way to worship, something harder to maintain in polytheistic cultures where virtues and vices were spread across a panoply of deities. Now political and religious obedience converged: a good Christian was also a good citizen.

This was a neat idea, later refined by Protestant and Catholic states during the Reformation. Unfortunately it was hard to enforce. Christianity attempted to separate divine and demonic power, which in practice meant prayer from magic, and *miracula* (God's miracles) from *mira* (demonic illusions). But ordinary people were unwilling or unable to grasp such distinctions; their religion was practical rather than abstract, rooted in quotidian routines and hazards. Cults, rituals, and private observance, often linked to Graeco-Roman deities, were all valuable ways to seek protection from fire, flood, and crop failure. In most communities, certain individuals were respected (and feared) as specialists able to dispense helpful magic. What could be done with these miscreants? Early in the 5th century, Rome tightened its legal code pertaining to magic, and Augustine of Hippo's *De Civitate Dei* ('City of God'), a seminal Christian tract, taught that pagan gods were demons and that magicians drew upon satanic power whether they realized it or not. On the ground, however, things looked different: old attitudes were too entrenched. Popular religion blurred lines between Christianity, paganism, and magic to produce a uniquely vigorous social resource.

Consequently, the early Christian church expressed hostility to magic but in practice was tolerant. Between the 6th and 9th centuries, reformers worked to absorb paganism, infusing old beliefs and rites with new meanings. Uniformity remained a political ideal. In AD 786, Charlemagne's law prohibiting conquered Saxons worshipping their gods was framed as an ordinance against devil-worship. Frankish victory was consolidated theologically and ideologically. The extra-terrestrial framework of this struggle for territory and power saw Christian soldiers locked in combat with demons and their earthly servants. This idea crystallized early in the 10th century with the *Canon Episcopi*, a definitive ruling of the church. Previously the Manichaean habit of treating God and Satan as opposing equals had tended to predominate, but here a different picture emerges. Everything in the universe now sprang from divine providence. Certain degenerates, it was claimed, abandoned God and as a consequence adhered to Satan, thus causing their spiritual damnation. Practitioners were to be exhibited as exempla of wickedness, then banished from Christian society. In this way, more than ever before, witchcraft and magic became linked to apostasy and heresy.

3. 'Sorcery in the School of Satan'. From John Lydgate's 1426 translation of Guillaume de Deguileville's mid-14th-century work *The Pilgrimage of the Life of Man*

Between the 11th and 13th centuries, the concept of witchcraft developed in two interconnected ways. First, as European intellectual life flowered, nourished by classical learning, so did interest in astrology, alchemy, and ritual magic. But the search for knowledge could not advance without considering the power that supplied it. Could this really be a Christian practice? Was high magic not sacrilegious, demonic even? The second development was the changing profile of Satan. The more deeply scholarly magicians probed universal mysteries, the more morbid the fear that they were devilish necromancers. The Devil mutated into a monstrous and aggressive figure whose ministrations were personal and intimate. This was the Satan of the New Testament rather than the Old: an explicit adversary to Christ and commander-in-chief of heretics and sorcerers. The thought followed that some of these deviants had sex with him. A 13th-century bishop of Paris believed Lucifer appeared to his followers 'in the form of a black cat or a toad demanding kisses from them, whether as a cat abominably under the tail, or as a toad horribly on the mouth'.

The war on witchcraft involved manipulating definitions and projecting images. Take the Cathars and the Waldensians. These French dissidents from orthodox Catholicism, both with 12th-century roots, were persecuted as sinister anti-Christians in league with Satan. Rumours about subversive Jewish rituals rubbed off too. We might see only ruthless kings and clerics here, cynically advancing power through terror. But the honour of Christ and the integrity of Christendom were infinitely precious, and had to be defended against threats that seemed very real. Convergence of the apostate and the magician, heretic, and witch, was not necessarily contrived: the associations flowed together, charged by social, economic, religious, and intellectual energies. The same applies to terminology. The Hebrew *kasaph* who, according to Exodus 22:18, deserved to die was a diviner; but in Latin versions of the text – *Maleficos non patieris vivere* – this acquired a diabolic meaning. In the English King James Bible (1611), the preferred translation was 'thou shalt not suffer a *witch* to live', reflecting the contemporary reality of witchcraft as a crime. In the Jacobean state, crown and subjects alike defended themselves with language, logic, and the law.

Mocking demonology as the dross of pre-Enlightenment thought, a feverish obsession of mad monks and paranoid princes, satisfies cravings for narratives about rational progress but misses the point. So does the notion that 'demonologist' was some kind of academic specialism or profession. Demonology was less a subject in itself than an intellectual resource employed in many respectable fields and debates, and not at all eccentric or fantastical. The historian Stuart Clark made a brilliant study of this called *Thinking with Demons* – a title which perfectly sums up the idea.

Secrecy and conspiracy

By 1500, the Church feared that a depraved, clandestine cult was engaged in anti-Christian conspiracy. The belief that heresy was satanic and organized owed much to hostility towards Waldensians. In the 1430s, an inquisitor in the duchy of Savoy wrote a treatise entitled *Errores Gazariorum* – 'Errors of the Cathars or Waldensians'. This describes in grisly detail the society of heretics, demonstrating that the secret nocturnal congregation – or 'sabbat' – was perfectly conceived before it joined the iconography of witchcraft. Upon swearing loyalty and a devotion to malice, it was said, the initiate 'adores the presiding devil and pays homage to him; and as a sign of homage kisses the devil, whether the devil appears as a human or some kind of animal, on the anus'. Before long, the shameful kiss, or *osculum infame*, mentioned by the bishop of Paris two centuries earlier, would be uniquely associated with witches, as would other related features such as aerial flight, deadly ointments made from infant corpses, and the tendency for most practitioners to be women.

These ideas crept out of the ivory towers and into the courts. In 1428, a mass trial of people fitting the heretic-witch stereotype took place in an Alpine region of Switzerland. Although learned demonology and the mechanisms of the law were essential factors, so too was the distress of farmers ruined by harvest failure. By the

4. German witches at a sabbat. A woman stoops to deliver the 'shameful kiss' to Satan, who has manifested in the form of a goat

time the *Errores Gazariorum* was written, a scatter of witch-trials occurred each year. Between the 1480s and 1520s, Europeans were afflicted by mortality crises which combined with fears about diabolic heresy and imminent Apocalypse in deadly synergy. In these decades, witches were tried in France, Italy, Spain, Germany,

21

Switzerland, and the Netherlands. A witch-hunt in the diocese of Como was particularly ferocious: a Dominican friar recorded that the Inquisition arrested 1,000 suspects a year, executing one in ten. Early in the 16th century, a healer who claimed to have acquired his powers in a land of fairies and witches triggered an investigation by the bishop of Trent, with the outcome that he, like twenty other suspects, was burned at the stake.

Notice how, for all its excesses, the Como tribunal was not out of control: instead, a 10% execution rate suggests caution about witchcraft. Our medieval ancestors were not the addle-brained bigots some make them out to be. Here we also discover an antagonism in witchcraft that maintained its tension as a judicial concept. First, as a conspiracy against God and man, witchcraft was extremely dangerous and demanded decisive action; second, due to its invisibility, it demanded great circumspection and discretion. This difficulty lay at the heart of printed treatises appearing at this time. Most notorious was the *Malleus Maleficarum*, or 'Hammer of the Witches', published in 1486. The author, a Dominican inquisitor named Heinrich Kramer, mixed demonological theory with first-hand experience, elevating peasant beliefs to cosmic significance while grounding academic theories in real life. By these means, it was hoped, demons might be condemned not just in print, but in the courts via their flesh-and-blood representatives: the witches.

The sabbat was a tricky idea, simultaneously the perfect illustration of the witch's wickedness, but almost never the substance of legal proof unless a suspect confessed to having attended one. Kramer avoided the subject, although he had plenty to say about who witches were, what they did, and the diabolic plot against Christian society. Underpinning this was an implicit attack not just on satanists, but on dualistic heretics – the heirs to Catharism – who believed in the war between an evenly matched God and Devil. Regular Christians maintained that God was supreme but allowed the Devil to tempt sinners to their own destruction and to assail other Christians, all of whom were flawed and deserved to be challenged and chastened. This intellectual device would remain central to how witchcraft was understood and resisted in Europe for the next three centuries. The sabbat was where witches were deceived as well as corrupted; in the end, the Devil was just a liar who promised wealth and power but was unable to deliver. The sin of his acolytes consisted in their spiritual weakness and cupidity.

It's not very historical to call Heinrich Kramer a superstitious psychopath, but he was up that end of the medieval spectrum. Both theologian and inquisitor, he relied not just on the Bible and Christian thinkers (as well as on classical authorities), but on his own labours at the sharp end. Procuring a special papal bull to silence critics, Kramer conducted investigations in the Tyrol, breaking every procedural rule, especially concerning torture. This campaign only increased opposition until the bishop of Brixen brought matters to a halt. Kramer's defence, a rambling if involving synthesis of demonological meditations and tall tales, became the *Malleus Maleficarum*, reprinted many times, though never as influential in its own era as it would be in the antagonistic climate of the Reformation and Counter-Reformation.

Neither an original contribution to debate nor the witch-hunter's handbook, the *Malleus* none the less established the idea that witches were lewd criminals to be hounded to their deaths in the secular courts, suspending legal convention if necessary. He also focused attention on the feminine identity of suspects. In sum, argued Kramer, four things were required of witches:

> they renounce the Catholic Faith in whole or part with a sacrilegious speech, solemnly devote themselves in body and soul, offer babies not yet reborn [i.e. unbaptized] to the Evil One, and persistently engage in the Devil's filthy deeds through carnal acts with incubus and succubus demons.

The projected world of the witches was therefore part object-lesson about sin, part millennial jeremiad, part febrile sexual fantasy, part early modern horror film. It repelled and it attracted; it fermented a heady brew of concern, fear, entertainment, and titillation. In the dead of night, on a hillside near you, women respecting no master but Satan congregated to pay homage, to gorge and fornicate, to hatch evil schemes – the very idea was as impossible to ignore as it was hard to evince with hard facts.

In 1673, a Northumbrian maidservant named Anne Armstrong confessed to magistrates that she had been lured to a sabbat where covens of thirteen witches danced for Satan and were treated to a sumptuous feast. In the annals of English witchcraft such evidence was rare, and in Armstrong's case rather naively bucolic: no boiled infants, shameful kisses, or incestuous orgies here. One historian has likened the sabbat described in continental confessions to 'a perverted village fair'. As we'll see, once demonology started being tested at law, there was only so long that such testimony, exotic and homespun at the same time, could possibly support it.

And yet the idea of the sabbat did not disappear after the witch-trials, nor were inquisitors and peasants its final custodians. In the 1920s, the mythologist Margaret Murray wrote a book claiming that persecuted witches had been a real pagan sect devoted to a horned god whom they worshipped secretly in covens. Although backed by little evidence, her theories were influential. Murray offered not only respite from the 'liberal-rationalist' idea that all witch-hunters were benighted sadists, but a naturalistic explanation to refute the outlandish idea, still current in some circles, that witches had truly compacted with Satan. A prominent exponent of this belief was Montague Summers, an eccentric Catholic writer once described as 'a mixture of spooks and sex and God'. In a work of 1928, Summers devoted a chapter to the sabbat, 'the ceremonial of hell', concluding that 'witches do actually and individually attend the sabbat, an orgy of blasphemy and obscenity'. Like Heinrich Kramer, whose *Malleus Maleficarum* he was the first to translate into English, Summers drew upon experience as well as learning. He had attended a black mass in 1913 and understood the allure.

Some historians criticized Margaret Murray, but most ignored her. As a result, her romantic (and therefore popular) take on medieval and early modern witches was allowed to flourish, most vividly in the invented traditions of the 20th-century neo-pagan movement. New scholarship from the 1960s delivered a frontal assault on Murray (d. 1963), but this was met with warnings about throwing the baby out with the bathwater. Carlo Ginzburg uncovered trials in the Italian region of Friuli, where 'witches' confessed to nighttime gatherings, seen by their inquisitors as diabolic sabbats. Ginzburg suggested that the *benandanti*, as they were known, men and women who believed their spirits left their bodies to fight demons, belonged to an agrarian fertility cult, as described by Murray. A second book, *Ecstasies*, dug through the deposited layers of an idea in search of the cultural origins of the sabbat. Both Ginzburg's works have been criticized for their wishful thinking, and for neglecting the social and intellectual contexts of archival material – the same charges levelled at Murray.

The world never did heed Montague Summers' warning of an expanding satanic empire; he ended his days in Oxford, teased in the street by students. He did, however, make an unexpected but lasting impression on Western culture. The rituals he described fed into a generation of horror writing, exemplified by the novels of Dennis Wheatley and the films they inspired. *The Devil Rides Out* (book, 1934; film, 1968), in which a group of friends gets caught up in a devil-cult, is a classic example. The infernal lyrics and bombastic stage-antics of heavy metal bands have also drawn on this tradition. The spoof 'rockumentary' *This is Spinal Tap* (1984) indulged in all sorts of pseudo-pagan nonsense, sending up a genre that never took itself that seriously anyway. The peculiar cultural power of witchcraft, however, is that it can entertain even while elsewhere it is cited as a cause of harm. The same 17th-century audiences which laughed at the topsy-turvy mischief of witches on the stage were sufficiently worried about real witches to hang them. Kramer may even have intended parts of the *Malleus* to be funny – gallows humour lost on us through the passage of time.

So much for early modern ambiguity of the horrific and the humorous. In the 1980s, child sex-abuse scandals, often alleging a ritual satanic element, rocked Britain and the United States. The scandal was that incompetent doctors, paranoid courts, and a hysterical media caused hundreds of innocent people to be investigated and even prosecuted; children were taken into care. The panic spread to Canada, Australia, New Zealand, the Netherlands, and Norway, and did not subside until the mid-1990s. The same details cropped up repeatedly: sexual perversions, incest, blood-sacrifice – things familiar not only to Montague Summers but to Heinrich Kramer. Perhaps we shouldn't be surprised. In the early 1980s, a survey found that 70% of Americans believed in the existence of diabolic cults preying on children.

Perhaps in the aftermath of the attacks in September 2001, the English-speaking world needs these paranoid myths more than ever, whether it realizes it or not. Even though the cultural 'other' is no longer couched in the precise idiom of the demonologists, we remain vulnerable to fears that secret forces may be working against us – an 'axis of evil' conspiring to destroy Western civilization.

Chapter 3
Malice

Healers and hags

Definitions of witchcraft vary but dictionaries don't really explain why; we have to dig deeper into actual experience. It may be that witchcraft's many forms resist pithy description because they existed primarily as sensations and images, retained unconsciously or subvocally. Even when private thoughts about witches were made public, formal principles and definitions were relatively unimportant: no peasant needed the *Malleus Maleficarum* to know that he was bewitched. Ideas were lived and felt: Wittgenstein's dictum 'meaning is use' applies to action as well as to speech. Nor did a profusion of meanings necessarily cause conflict or contradiction. In the spheres of daily life (household, parish, courtroom, etc.), contrasting images of witchcraft co-existed in dynamic, creative tension. Witches, therefore, were cultural hybrids, blending learned and popular traditions.

Neither tradition translated directly into practice, partly because each was inconsistent in itself. As we saw earlier, modulation in meaning occurred whenever distinctions were actively forced: elites ignoring folk magic or extirpating it as blasphemy; the common people regarding magicians as helpful healers or horrible hags. In parish life, Glenda the Good easily morphed into Wanda the Wicked. To make sense of this, we need to get inside some real witchcraft accusations. According to the historian Michael MacDonald, 'stories are really all we have to reconstruct the inner lives of people in the past; stories are what they were made from in the first place'.

Let's take two women from the mid-16th century. Elizabeth Mortlock lived in Pampisford, a Cambridgeshire farming community; Appoline Behr was a miner's wife from Sainte-Marie, an upland village in the duchy of Lorraine. Both were healers, untrained and unlicensed, ordinary women hauled from obscurity when they were accused of witchcraft. These excursions left marks on the historical record, Mortlock's among the Ely Diocesan Records in Cambridge University Library, and Behr's in the Archives Départementales de Meurthe-et-Moselle at Nancy.

In June 1566, a church court heard that Elizabeth Mortlock healed children and animals, and diagnosed people possessed by spirits. She used Christian prayers: 'five Paternosters in the worship of the five wounds of our Lord; five Aves in the worship of the five joys of our Lady; and one Creed in the worship of the blessed Father, the Son and the Holy Ghost and the holy twelve Apostles, in the vulgar tongue'. Praying in English, like reading vernacular bibles, was central to Protestant conversion after the Reformation. But these were Catholic prayers, condemned as superstitious, especially when used for profane ends. Such healing could *not* be worked through God, as Mortlock claimed, so it must be devilish. Of course, she, and presumably her patients, believed she did nothing but good. Europe teemed with practitioners supplying not just medicine but divination, prophecy, and counter-magic. Mortlock was charged with unorthodox devotion, a sin which in a polarized religious culture diverted the gaze from Christ to Satan. The court ordered her to stand before the congregation, wearing a white sheet and a placard reading 'for wicked witchcraft worthily I bid rebuke and shame'.

Mortlock was branded a witch, not because she had physically embraced the Devil as described in the demonologies but because the Church had labelled her as deviant. When Appoline Behr was denounced as a witch, the consequences were more severe. Having successfully treated ailments with incantations, ointments, and rituals, she fell out with some clients, perhaps because she over-charged them. When they became ill, and in some cases died, she fell under suspicion. Behr was, after all, believed to be magically adept at manipulating health and sickness, life and death; that was why people consulted her. Interrogated in December 1580, she denied witchcraft, but under torture finally confessed to compacting with an evil spirit. This completed her transmutation from good witch to bad witch, and she was executed early in 1581.

Tales like this reveal more than simple typologies ever can. On the ground, meanings were motile and mutable. Whereas one anthropologist might conflate sorcery and witchcraft in modern sub-Saharan Africa, defining both as low magic, another would insist that the former serves positive ends, the latter negative ones; yet another might distinguish between freely available magic and special innate powers. Distinctions are unfixed. What the *subjects* of anthropology think may lie permanently out of reach, or at least beyond accurate expression in any language including their own.

Gender complicates things. Nowadays we think of witches as female, warlocks or wizards their male counterparts. But originally 'warlock' meant 'oath-breaker' and only acquired a diabolic twist in 16th-century Scotland; wizards were wise women and men, then high magicians, before they became witches. The term 'witch', meanwhile, comes from the Old English verb *wiccian*, meaning to cast spells, without preference for gender. A male practitioner was a *wicca*, the female *wicce*. In early modern England, 'witch' applied to both men and women, although by then it had taken on a fiercely negative meaning, closer to the Latin term *maleficus*. Most people called white witches 'cunning folk', or wise women and men; to them a 'witch' was exclusively a hate-filled maleficent woman or, as in one case in five, a man.

To say that one-fifth of English witchcraft suspects were male is another way of saying 80% were female. The fact that Mortlock and Behr were women is significant, not because female healers were systematically persecuted – they were not – but because their work led them into relationships which made them vulnerable to accusation. At the same time, witchcraft was associated with women because they were seen as the 'weaker vessel', more susceptible to diabolic temptation. The original here was Eve. Misogyny, hatred of women, was a negative mutation of the more positive concept of patriarchy: rule by male householders. Seventeenth-century men didn't hate women, but the notion that female wilfulness threatened society quickly surfaced in times of crisis. Women's bodies were considered inversions or corruptions of the male ideal, their constitutions unstable, their desires menacing. When the world flipped upside down, women would straddle their menfolk, reins in hand. To dream of nocturnal assault by a witch was to be 'hag-ridden'.

Links between women and witchcraft date back to antiquity. Wicked female magicians were known to the Egyptians and Babylonians. The Sumerians feared Lilitu (the Hebrew Lilith), a shrieking demon in the form of a barren and envious woman. Classical texts developed the theme. The body-snatching witches described by Horace were female; Homer related how the sorceress Circe turned Odysseus's sailors into pigs and taught him how to converse with the dead. Medea, subject of Euripides' tragedy, was known for various maleficent acts, including killing a love-rival with a magic robe. She was also a priestess of Hecate, that malevolent goddess who, with Circe, was the salient model of the female witch into the Renaissance. The Bible, too, featured a number of sorceresses, famously the 'Witch of Endor', who conjured up the spirit of Samuel for Saul.

5. Henry Fuseli's *The Nightmare*, c. 1781. A demon squats on the chest of the sleeping woman, observed by a wild-eyed horse

In reality, ancient men were just as likely to engage in conjuring spirits, cooking up potions, healing and harming; but that only makes it more interesting that the theoretical witch, the literary witch, the witch of popular imagination, should be female. The polarity of gender and the polarity of good and evil were, perhaps unconsciously, aligned, so that the mysteries of womanhood lent substance to the mystery of what it meant to be a witch.

Vengefulness and spite, unbridled female sexuality, and unholy spiritual power were thus intimately connected.

Christian demonization of pagan deities was influenced by gender. Diana, Roman goddess of the moon, represented nocturnal female power; the survival of her cult inspired Margaret Murray's flights of fancy. The 10th-century *Canon Episcopi* condemned 'wicked women [who], perverted by the Devil...believe and profess themselves, in the hours of night, to ride upon certain beasts with Diana'. Diana was also equated with Holda, a German goddess of motherhood identified as a witch by theologians and lawyers. This all strengthened the idea of the witch as a furtive, self-governing woman, drawing down power that was not Christian so had to be demonic. The *Malleus Maleficarum* focused this image, piling on reasons why most witches were women, including their gullibility, garrulousness, carnality, and infidelity. Independence was dangerous. 'When a woman thinks alone', warned Kramer, 'she thinks evil thoughts'. In the 16th century, with the cult of the Virgin promoted by Counter-Reformation rulers, the anti-type of Eve was replaced by that of the witch, who more exactly represented the negation of the divine covenant and beneficent motherhood.

The timing of the main witch-hunt, between the 16th and 18th centuries, has been linked to growing concern about female conduct. Economic change, especially capitalism and commercialization, may have elevated the public profile of women in a way that infected the male imagination, resulting in a 'gender crisis'. The idea shouldn't be taken too far; it definitely doesn't mean that witch-hunting was a masculine conspiracy against uppity women, as some have claimed. We can be more certain that the female witch-stereotype was established by 1500, even if, as in the ancient world, ordinary people were not constrained by it in daily life. Ultimately, witches were pursued because they were *witches*, not because they were women. But if we could go back and ask a Tudor bystander to describe a witch, you could be fairly sure he or she would say a malevolent woman with diabolic powers. And, as defamation cases illustrate, 'witch' was an insult specific to women, like 'whore' or 'bitch'.

Slander trials show that witchcraft could be a name without a deed as well as, quoting Macbeth's witches again, a deed without a name. Witchcraft was rooted in language as well as feeling, and words could constitute witchcraft without need for any act to have occurred. Speech, seen as a female counterpart to male physical force, possessed destructive or otherwise transformative power – the overt imprecation or the inference of meaning from innocuous but ambiguous remarks. As recently as the 1970s, the ethnographer Jeanne Favret-Saada found that in the Bocage region of western France, where magical beliefs thrived, 'in witchcraft, words wage war'. Furthermore, this oral culture left 'no room for uninvolved observers'. Merely by asking questions, Favret-Saada became tangled in a dense web of memory, gossip, suspicion, and local politics. This, too, had been the world of the 16th century.

Age also connected women with witchcraft. The elderly were marginal, vulnerable, and overwhelmingly female. Many had lost the framework of family support that enabled younger women to resist enemies. The Elizabethan sceptic Reginald Scot noticed that most people's idea of a witch was a woman who was 'old, lame, blear-eyed, pale, foul, and full of wrinkles', usually a widow dependent on charity who 'waxeth odious and tedious to her neighbours'. Here we identify a source of the failed trust, brooding resentment, and hardening convictions that caused the downfall of Appoline Behr and many like her. And who is to say that paranoia about the impoverished woman next door may not have had its counterpart in the mind of the suspect herself? Given the pervasive reality of early modern witch-beliefs, she might have seen in magic an opportunity to settle scores and for once to get ahead in her miserable life.

The damage done

In 2004, workmen digging in Greenwich, near London, uncovered a sealed stone bottle that rattled and splashed when they shook it. It was sent to a laboratory where X-rays revealed metal objects wedged in the neck, suggesting that it had been buried upside down, and a scan showed it to be half filled with liquid. Chemical analysis confirmed this was human urine containing nicotine and brimstone. When the cork was removed, scientists discovered iron nails, brass pins, hair, fingernail parings, a pierced leather heart, and what they believed might be navel fluff.

What had gone through the mind of whoever buried that bottle? Without doubt it was a magical device, dating from the first half of the 17th century; less well preserved examples have been found throughout England. But whether it was intended as protection against witchcraft or the means to reverse a spell, we'll never know. The heart-charm suggests other possibilities: perhaps love magic, or even that the user had wished harm on someone. Sticking pins in pictures and models is part of witches' stock-in-trade. In 1962, parishioners at Castle Rising in Norfolk discovered human effigies and a thorn-studded sheep's heart nailed to their church door. Presumably this was not just a blasphemous insult but a specific physical attack. If so, it belonged to an ancient tradition of popular *maleficium* – real in intent if not in effect, but hard to recover historically because of its covert nature.

We tend to see witchcraft as a delusion, a non-existent crime, because we reject its mechanics. This is why many believe executed witches to have been innocent. Yet we still punish those who attempt crimes but fail, and a legal distinction exists between *mens rea* and *actus reus*: the thought and the deed. Surely some early modern people must have *tried* to kill with magic; it would be incredible if they hadn't. Seen in context, was attempted murder by witchcraft not a crime, just as a woman devoted to Satan was an apostate even if she had never actually met him? There was a lot of

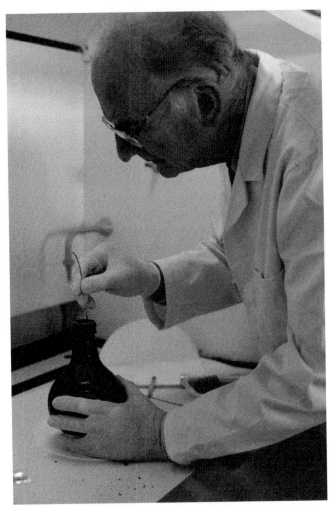

6. A scientist looks inside a 'witch-bottle' discovered in Greenwich in 2004

magic in our ancestors' lives, and positive forces could be turned into negatives. Plus there is an exception to the rule that *maleficium* is hard for historians to recover: widespread counter-magic against malefic witches. The definition of witchcraft depended not on its inherent nature but on how it was applied. In 1684, one Englishman noted the irony that folk 'often become witches by endeavouring to defend themselves against witchcraft'.

In the ancient world, too, aggressive magic was more than just something the virtuous suspected of the wicked: it was a recognized source of personal power, albeit unlawful if used against a blameless opponent. From Mesopotamia, not only do illicit antisocial spells survive, but descriptions of official ceremonies in which images of assailing witches were burned. Excavations at Greek and Roman sites turn up curses scratched on scraps of lead known as *defixiones*. Some contain cloth or hair; occasionally they were buried in graves to inflict a deadening effect on victims. An example from Messina targeted 'the evil-doer' Valeria Arsinoe; 'sickness and decay attack the nymphomaniac!', read the malediction. Dolls made of lead, clay, or wax were also used. Egyptian examples can be seen in the Louvre and the British Museum, the former a trussed woman spiked with nails, the latter a torso containing a papyrus curse.

So the counter-magical laws of antiquity, like their Dark Age and medieval successors, did more than symbolically defend religious orthodoxy or swipe superstitiously at a non-existent enemy: they addressed a real crime. The *Canon Episcopi*, which was actually sceptical of most claims made by witches, forbade *sortilegium et maleficium* – not just village magic but cursing. Pre-modern rulers were responding to the plain fact that ordinary people tried to wreak havoc using magic.

Malefic magic can be studied first hand. Sir Edward Evans-Pritchard (1902–73), professor of social anthropology at Oxford, noticed the ordinariness of witchcraft among the Azande of the upper Nile; it was as uncontroversial as illness. Azande witch-beliefs included *bagbudma*: spiritual medicine that reversed bewitchment by attacking the witch. In the Roman spa at Bath, archaeologists found a lead curse deposited by a man whose cloak had been stolen; the Azande, too, had a spell for thieves: 'May misfortune come upon you, thunder roar, seize you, and kill you. May a snake bite you so that you die. May death come upon you from ulcers' – and so on. Such magic upheld positive social values. J. D. Krige described a 'moral grading of magic' among the Lobedu of the Transvaal, who condoned supernatural vengeance – or *madabi* – against witches but criminalized malicious usage. 'The power is in itself neutral', explained Krige, 'it is the objective which makes it moral or immoral'. The Shona of Zimbabwe encourage sorcery against enemies while forbidding it in their 'moral community'. In 1983, a student in Cameroon confessed to membership of a gang of night sorcerers – reminiscent of Siberian shamans or Ginzburg's *benandanti* – who had symbolically eaten their teacher's heart.

The concept of *maleficium* may strike outsiders as an error, but to insiders it feels more like a rational reaction to danger. This perception may be reinforced by something we find particularly difficult to accept: the possibility of literally frightening someone to death. Voodoo is a religion of Haiti, syncretizing African beliefs and Roman Catholicism. Followers worship *loa*, gods or spirits condemned as demons by the Church. Haitians do believe in black magic, although its more gross aspects – raising the dead, aerial flight, shape-shifting – have been exaggerated by horror movies. A major influence on public perceptions was the 1973 film *Live and Let Die*, where voodoo adds intrigue to James Bond's Caribbean exploits. And yet real voodoo rituals can be terrifying, generating an intoxicating energy beyond what seems human and natural. The travel writer Patrick Leigh Fermor witnessed an initiation ceremony, the *Brûler Zin*, complete with sacrifices and incantations, that wouldn't have looked out of place in the *Malleus Maleficarum*. 'The cauldrons and the flames, the flying feathers, the blood, the ring of serious black faces in the firelight', Fermor recalled, 'were a wild and disquieting sight'. Channelled through witch-doctors and aimed at credulous individuals, the psychological effect could be traumatic.

We return here to an earlier theme: fear. The Scientific Revolution is often seen as a barrier in mentalities between us and our witch-believing ancestors. But just as significant was the Industrial Revolution, which in the end delivered a liberating prosperity, freeing most Westerners from fear: fear of starvation, of bitter competition with neighbours, of minor ailments and diseases, and of the loss of uninsured property. If you can imagine leading a life of near destitution and dependence on capricious fortune, you're on your way to understanding the social reality of witchcraft. The idea of *maleficium* is hardly more alien than the suffering and emotion that sustain it.

Again, stories lead us to the truth. In 1645, Annabel Durrant from the Essex village of Fingringhoe informed magistrates that Mary Johnson had poisoned her two-year-old son with bread and butter, and that he had taken eight days to die. Durrant's grief was so extreme she felt it as physical pain – like childbirth, she said. She saw Johnson's apparition, an experience so petrifying that she lost her speech and use of her arms. Persuaded to testify, Durrant gained a little strength only to see her husband struck down with chest pains; shortly afterwards part of their house collapsed. It seems that the Durrants' bereavement and fear had mutated into psychosomatic illness and near hysteria. Perhaps the Greenwich resident who, 400 years ago, sealed a voodoo heart in a stone bottle was consumed by similar passions.

Historians of witchcraft are not keen on the concept of hysteria. Like evil, it's too crude and undifferentiating, too resistant to substantiation; it lets us off explaining what really happened. Sometimes, though, hysteria is the only word for it; it's surely what we would say were we transported to Fingringhoe in 1645, or indeed to Salem, Massachusetts, in 1692. At this most famous of all witch-trials, one of the accused, Bridget Bishop, was unable to satisfy her interrogator, pleading innocence as spectators murmured and possessed girls wailed around the courtroom. 'Do you not see how they are tormented?', bellowed Judge Hathorne. 'You are acting witchcraft before us? What do you say to this? Why have you not a heart to confess the truth?'

Parental fear was the cornerstone of both stories. Early modern people were perfectly able to explain misfortune, including sickness in children, without their minds leaping to witchcraft; divine or natural causation was normal. As Evans-Pritchard said of the Azande: 'the world known to the senses is just as real to them as it is to us'. So what was it about certain instances of misfortune that bred suspicions of witchcraft? In the first place, particular social conditions and relations created optimal conditions for believing in the magical malice of neighbours. Secondly, some misfortunes seemed bizarre, undeserved, or both. Annabel Durrant might have accepted the loss of her son had he passed away peacefully; what made the difference was that she had watched him writhe in agony for eight days. Providence took children suddenly from their mothers; it did not torture them to death. As Einstein remarked, 'God is subtle but he is not malicious'.

Loathe thy neighbour

To mark the retirement of Evans-Pritchard in 1968, a conference was held in Oxford. Among the speakers was Keith Thomas, a historian in the university writing about popular religion in early modern England. He had recently supervised a doctoral thesis on witchcraft in Essex by Alan Macfarlane whose thinking, like Thomas's own, had been influenced by the anthropology to which Evans-Pritchard had contributed so much. Thomas's paper, and books he and Macfarlane published in the early 1970s, started a debate about the value of the comparative method. The main objection centred on context. England in the 17th century and modern Africa had similar witch-beliefs; but the cultures in which belief was embedded, and from which it derived meaning, were chalk and cheese. 'Non-Western social anthropology provides keys that do not fit European locks', warned one historian of French witchcraft.

Evans-Pritchard might have been first to agree. The world of the Azande throws up correspondences with earlier European experience, but it deserves to be understood *sui generis* as a discrete culture. Differences are pronounced, as we might expect given the rootedness and complex connectivity of a people and their social setting. For example, Azande witchcraft accusations did not ride a wave of emotion; they seemed more like 'the fulfilment of a pious duty', acts of commitment and conviction dispassionately executed. Compare this with the anguished furore surrounding the trials of Mary Johnson and Bridget Bishop. In pre-industrial Europe, fear and loathing were the order of the day. Witches were often believed to be angry; but almost invariably suspects made their neighbours angry, and unusually so.

The lethal intensity of this relationship came from competition and conflict. In the Middle Ages, royal and aristocratic power struggles often involved allegations of witchcraft. Edward II was apt to accuse opponents. In the 1320s, Dame Alice Kyteler was tried at Kilkenny for malefic murder and demonism, thus ending a feud between noble Irish families. She escaped to England, minus her property, which passed to her accusers. It has been suggested that witch-trials (for instance, in New England) were a means to appropriate wealth, but most witches were dirt-poor. Besides which, like hysteria, this explains witchcraft away without tackling the difficult matter of belief. Too easily we fall into the trap of saying what witchcraft was *really* about, as if the idea that an accusation might *really* be about witchcraft is unacceptable. That the prosecution of Elizabeth Mortlock, healer of Pampisford, may have been a factional vendetta – unusually that year no one from her family served as churchwarden – doesn't mean her behaviour was not genuinely offensive to orthodox Protestants. In pre-modern England, as in modern Africa, people cooked up false accusations; but without a bedrock of reality to witch-beliefs these charges would have made no sense.

Cynical stratagem or act of faith, witchcraft, like war, was politics by other means. The foundations of European beliefs and suspicions, dating back to Mesopotamia, were land and resources: scarcity of food and fuel, difficulty in sustaining independent households, the fragility of rural economies, and consequent volatility in social relations. Farming was a fixed existence, locking people into intimate and intense relationships; these bonds were vital for survival but often fell short of ideals of charity and cooperation. In this world, politics were not restricted to the elite: what really mattered were the 'politics of the parish'. Testimony against the healer Appoline Behr reveals a tightly woven mesh of associations – affinities and animosities – that added up to her being manoeuvred out of the community and into oblivion. Robin Briggs describes Lorraine as a holistic spiritual and physical environment where witch-beliefs were endemic but accusations emerged from intricate patterns of causation. Pressures built up slowly but surely. The ties that bound neighbours were strong, but often these exerted an equal and opposite force elsewhere in the community.

Crises accentuated what happened even in years of relative calm. Towards the mid-2nd century AD, the prosperity of the Roman Empire dissolved into depression and unemployment, leading to increased persecution of Christians accused of black magic and other crimes that angered the gods. The purges at Lyons in AD 177 exemplify this. In early modern Europe, demographic growth caused catastrophic levels of inflation, poverty, and social dislocation, a drama played out in communities across the continent. Like the 2nd century, the 16th was also scarred by rebellion and war, further destabilizing political and economic relations. Climate change did the rest.

The early modern era roughly coincided with the 'Little Ice Age', a period of unusually cool and wet weather damaging to crops and livestock. Early signs appeared in the 15th century, especially the 1420s and 1480s, when the demonization of heresy first erupted into witch-hunting. But the climatic descent grew steeper around 1560 when sustained prosecutions began, reaching a nadir around 1590 when many states experienced agrarian crisis and witch-hunting. This was also an age of epidemic disease of a severity not seen since the Black Death in the mid-14th century. In Geneva, Milan, and other cities, diabolical 'plague-spreaders' (in French, *engraisseurs*) were executed, just as today in Zambia the explosion of AIDS is blamed on witches. Many African states are blighted by extreme poverty; competition for resources breeds enmity between communities and within. Under these conditions, witchcraft has been seen as a 'social strain-gauge', or safety valve. Witchcraft accusations are much rarer among nomads and the inhabitants of dispersed settlements. In tribal societies where disputes are solved by splitting rather than confrontation, malefic witchcraft is virtually unknown.

A range of emotions lie behind early modern witchcraft accusations. Fear, anger, and hatred, for sure; but also envy – in the words of Wolfgang Behringer, 'one of the most basic negative feelings on an anthropological Richter scale of emotions'. Azande whom Evans-Pritchard tried to befriend fretted they would be bewitched by neighbours jealous of his friendship. Good fortune disrupted established economic patterns. Pliny the Elder told of a farmer, a manumitted slave, accused of witchcraft by neighbours resentful and suspicious of his plentiful harvests. African hunters say that finding two honeycombs in the forest is lucky; to find three is witchcraft. So long as they are not over-developed into explanatory schemes, comparative history and anthropology can be illuminating.

Rather than childishly jealous, these Romans and Africans exhibited some serious if indistinct economic thinking. In witchcraft we see how individual feelings interacted with collective custom, part of the advanced circuitry of a full-blown accusation. This takes us back to the idea of 'zero-sum gain', or 'limited good': the subsistence farmer's unconscious appreciation of the 'moral economy': predictable demand and supply, with a finite quantity of wealth and resources more or less equally shared – a fair equilibrium. Investment, profit, and economic growth were not widely held ideals prior to the Industrial Revolution. Even the puritan individualists colonizing New England were encouraged to seek a 'sufficiency' of land, and no more.

As the fleets were arriving in America, the situation in England was grim. In the century after 1540, the population roughly doubled, which, though tiny by modern standards, strained the economic infrastructure. The nation's agrarian base was designed for continuity not change, and the effects were felt by millions. Some made fortunes from inflation; many became slightly richer. But the majority found it harder to work, and earned less with which to buy (more expensive) food. Statutory parish relief kept the poor from starving but commodified their relationship with richer neighbours. Cultural rifts opened between people traditionally bound by good faith and custom, one side craving informal charity, the other increasingly reluctant to give it. The resulting emotions, respectively, were anger and guilt. This idea was most elegantly put forward by Alan Macfarlane and Keith Thomas, the latter incorporating the effect the Reformation had in condemning spiritual protection against witches.

The lasting influence of the so-called 'charity-refused' or 'refusal-guilt' thesis is due to the fact that Macfarlane and Thomas tackled the main problem of the anthropological models associated with Evans-Pritchard and others: explaining long-term change. The structures and rhythms of tribal life were continuous, a place where witch-beliefs fitted neatly. The European witch-hunt, however, happened in an era of radical discontinuity. Today historians decry grand transitional narratives, but feudalism *did* give way to capitalism; industrialism and urbanization *did* reshape rural lives; and rural custom *was* agonizingly erased. Perhaps the Oxford historians were too prescriptive – a new generation found many exceptions to their model, its applicability to continental states is dubious, and even Macfarlane changed his mind – but they successfully demonstrated that the rise of witchcraft accusations was a birthpang of modernity.

Social anthropology has come far since Evans-Pritchard, unlike relations between anthropologists and historians which seem as cool as ever. Today anthropologists of witchcraft are much concerned with the birthpangs of modernity. Since decolonization, many African countries have changed dramatically, not always for the better. Independence movements, for instance in Malawi and Zimbabwe, have expressed their ambitions through witch-hunting; from below, fear, malice, and economic crisis supply the requisite loathing between neighbours. Even in quieter regions like Tanzania, poor living standards, via modernization, have led to vicious bursts of witch-persecution. The title of Peter Geschiere's book, *The Modernity of Witchcraft*, says it all. Whereas once it seemed a good idea to explore the structure of early modern primitivism through that of 20th-century Africa, now parallels appear in the traumas of transition in both continents. Like 17th-century Europeans, modern educated Africans believe in witchcraft, suggesting that the witch's grip is more tenacious than we might think.

Chapter 4
Truth

Debating Satan

Witchcraft has many faces. We've seen contrasts not just between etic and emic standpoints – modern perspectives on the past, and the past on its own terms – but among historians (and anthropologists) and among contemporaries themselves. Romans and Greeks wondered whether 'good' *daimones* were bad after all; Christians wondered whether any magic was compatible with faith. There were no clear answers; or rather there were, but they could only be asserted as *a priori* truths, not proved by reason. Medieval theologians explained the dark arts in the same archaic way they explained the entire universe: deductively not inductively, proceeding *faithfully* from established causes to visible effects, rather than *empirically* from effects to causes. The existence of the Devil was a given: everything followed from that, albeit in a baffling welter of interpretations about demonic agency. In the 16th and 17th centuries, Protestant reformers inveighed against magic, but struggled to suppress it with teaching because it resided in the heart rather than the mind. Witch-beliefs are more visceral than cerebral.

It was impossible to leave witchcraft alone, however. The enquiry had to continue, and for two reasons. First, the Christian Church was embattled by heresy, then at the Reformation divided, indeed fragmented, by divergent faiths. One route to the desired monopoly of truth was demonology; it was a conceptual foil to doctrine – darkness making sense of the light – and a means to denigrate opponents. Competition motivated theologians to make better arguments; in the end, witchcraft came under more scrutiny than it could bear. The second reason was that orthodoxy in the populace was not upheld in the seminary or debating chamber, but in the law courts. This meant gathering and evaluating evidence likely to establish the truth of witchcraft – not a general philosophical truth, but the guilt or innocence of people on trial for their lives. The pressure to get this right was immense: shedding innocent blood cried out to heaven for revenge. But ultimately the task proved hopeless. Long before the Devil was banished from homes and neighbourhoods, legal evidence of his engagement with human beings was invalidated and witch-trials abandoned. The truth had changed.

The history of witchcraft illustrates the way that knowledge was not manufactured in a vacuum, but artfully determined by institutions and ideologies. Knowledge was political, and so therefore was witchcraft. Even among the masses, witchcraft accusations were shaped by material conditions and social relations, both the substance of politics. Hardly ever was the difference between belief and non-belief, truth and falsehood, simply a free choice between credulity and scepticism. It was difficult to free witchcraft from its social, religious, and political moorings because without them it had no substantive meaning. When the legal and evidential ties were cut, an entire dimension of its existence vanished and the early modern witch-hunt came to an end.

For classical and medieval thinkers to test the legitimacy of magic, they had to consider how it worked. By 1500, the argument that all magic was implicitly demonic, on the basis that no such power would ever flow from God, clearly needed refinement. How could a natural philosopher investigate God's arcane mysteries, and so glorify Him, without experiment? Science did not split from religion until the 19th century, and the desire to understand creation was its main characteristic. This was the 'providential tradition' in which men like Isaac Newton and Robert Boyle operated. But change came with preference for rational observation over slavish devotion to ancient wisdom. In the 1660s, Boyle criticized the deductive methodology of fellow chemists; for all their grandiose cosmological frameworks – perhaps because of them – their analyses were narrow and hackneyed, constrained by hallowed tradition. But then again Boyle practised alchemy, a morally questionable discipline involving angelic communication. What was the difference between summoning angels and conjuring demons, especially when, as the Bible taught, Satan himself may appear as 'an angel of light'?

Boyle was not alone in pursuing this agenda. His intellectual circle included Newton himself, whose theory of gravity was no more than an occult force exerted by one body upon another. Perhaps those Diana cults worshipping the moon hadn't been far wrong. And Newton was explicitly interested in alchemy, angels, and numerology (searching for hidden meanings in the Bible), fields of enquiry passed over by biographers who prefer him to be a scientist in the modern mould, but integral to his mentality and aims in the 17th century. 'Newton was not the first of the age of reason', commented the economist Keynes, but 'the last of the age of magicians'.

The Bible didn't help with this ambiguity. Not all its magicians were impious sorcerers like the Witch of Endor: some Jewish priests performed magic to demonstrate to rivals the power of Yahweh, and all manner of divination and cursing was condoned if done in His name. Early Christians were more hostile to magic, and explicit about defining it. But in many ways, and so far as peasant congregations were concerned, the priesthood absorbed and replicated magical rituals. It was still magic, but now it was *their* magic. What was a blessing if not a charm bestowed in God's

Truth

name? Meanwhile learned magicians proceeded on the basis that God's universe was full of mysteries and that they might reveal these to glorify Him. Hence a common thread runs between the mystics of Renaissance Neoplatonism and the virtuosi of the Scientific Revolution. Even so, distinguishing the providential from the demonic was difficult, and the Christian Church continued to define itself against Satan and the kingdom of darkness. In a polarized scheme that placed witches and heretics at one extreme and priests and theologians at the other, magicians were pushed closer to the former. The only indemnity was offered by high social status and, for a few, elite patronage.

Even here moral ambiguity was a problem. Dr Dee and Dr Lambe, Tudor and Stuart magicians respectively, demonstrate this. John Dee was an erudite and devout investigator of the occult. A fellow of Trinity College, Cambridge, he indulged in alchemy and conversations with angels. Like Newton, another Trinity man, he was both mathematician and magician, the line between the roles unclear. Dee advised Elizabeth I, and spent time at Rudolf II's court in Prague. It was a perilous existence. A horoscope to help a monarch might foretell a royal death: important service might become magical treason. Dee had been arrested for conjuration under Queen Mary, and had to flee from Emperor Rudolf; his library was ransacked, and in the 1590s he was blamed for demonic phenomena in London and accused of atheism. After 1600, he fell from favour and died in obscurity. John Lambe's career took off around this time. A disreputable conjurer, Lambe nevertheless secured the patronage of the king's favourite, the duke of Buckingham. In the end, however, public hostility to Buckingham was manifested as hostility to 'the duke's wizard', and both were murdered in 1628.

All knowledge was power, including arcane knowledge, so inevitably princely courts entertained men of skill and inclination, despite the risks. Astrology was another discipline stuck in the margin between science and witchcraft. During the English civil

war, William Lilly helped many clients, high and low, to see their
futures in the stars, but not without criticism: in 1652, he was
charged under the Witchcraft Act. More than one 17th-century
theologian insisted that astrology played into the hands of Satan,
who thrived on the vanity and curiosity of the unwary.

The greatest debt of modern science to the Renaissance and
Reformation was the way the truth was put into contention as
never before. By attacking the claims of the Catholic Church,
Protestant thinkers forced crucial distinctions between the divine
and the demonic, the religious and the magical, the sacred and the
profane. Although they never would have guessed it, their labours
resulted in what would later be called 'the disenchantment of the
world', when links between demons and humans were severed for
good, and burning someone for making such a connection could no
longer be justified. Truth came to follow the principles of the
present not the past.

How to find a witch

However coherent early modern demonology was as academic
theory, in practical application it was, according to Lyndal Roper,
'a morass of images, half-articulated convictions and contradictory
positions'. It was a mess, albeit rich with possibilities precisely
because there were so few testable certainties. The legal process,
however, demanded certainty: it aimed to find truth by inductive
methods. But if Europe's finest scholars couldn't prove witchcraft
with any lasting accuracy or consistency, what hope was there for
the majority whose testimony supplied judges and juries with the
substance of their deliberations? In any case, unlettered villagers
had their own ideas about demons and witches, and their own
ways of identifying them.

Early modern peasants were not obsessed with witches, but they
did spend time thinking and talking about them; every village had
its cunning folk and probably malefic suspects too. Prosecuting

them was another thing altogether: best just to stay out of their way (without being stand-offish). In an age of movement and uncertainty rumours travelled fast. Swedish soldiers returning from the Thirty Years War (1618–48) spread popular demonology in Scandinavia, and in 1629 Catholic cavalrymen in the German city of Rothenburg ob der Tauber infected locals with their overheated ideas and tried, unsuccessfully, to start a witch-hunt. In Elizabethan England, a Protestant bishop, formerly exiled under Mary I, counselled the new queen that witches 'are marvellously increased within this your grace's realm. These eyes have seen most evident and manifest marks of their wickedness. Your grace's subjects pine away even unto death; their colour fadeth, their flesh rotteth, their senses are bereft.'

Elizabeth I introduced witchcraft legislation in 1559 (not ratified until 1563), but in some of the earliest cases the accused were acquitted, suggesting that witnesses had failed to convince jurors. Possibility did not easily translate into certainty, and yet the gravity of the crime meant that demonology flourished throughout Europe, carried by the political and intellectual momentum of Reformation and Counter-Reformation. Preaching and print were important for communicating new concepts. Images of the Devil had been obliterated in Protestant churches, but now you could hear about him instead: he was real and he was coming for you – assisted by witches. Nor were images taboo if used appropriately. In Germany, Lutheran propaganda was disseminated in printed broadsides bearing woodcut illustrations of the Pope as a monstrous Antichrist.

Perhaps the greatest contribution of the *Malleus Maleficarum* was not in intellectual life but in iconography. Kramer's vivid descriptions helped to gather, fix, and broadcast visions of witchcraft as art. Albrecht Dürer's engraving *Witch Riding Backwards on a Goat* (c. 1500) depicts a post-menopausal hag in her pomp, breasts sagging and hair flying, calling in a hailstorm. *The Four Witches* (1497) shows the Devil wreathed in sulphur,

7. Albrecht Dürer's *Witch Riding Backwards on a Goat* (c. 1500)

spying on a naked gathering of his servants. These extravagant, profoundly sexualized images were developed by Dürer's apprentice Hans Baldung Grien, whose interpretation of a sabbat – a tight composition of witches, smoke, and magical paraphernalia – influenced other artists including Lucas Cranach, Luther's propagandist. Cranach's allegorical painting *Melancholia* (1533) juxtaposed the religious and moral corruption of witches and the Catholic clergy. Patrons and collectors demanded such art, and, like most fashions, tastes filtered down to the lower orders. The Reformation generated a profusion of cheap print, including news-sheets, pamphlets, and ballads about witches that both reflected and focused popular opinion. Some were even laid out like comic-strips to help humbler readers follow the story.

The stereotype of the female witch, particularly the malevolent crone, was thus powerfully reinforced. In most witch-trials, however, misfortunes were not randomly blamed on women who looked like witches, but fitted into specific patterns of social relations involving conflict and fear between neighbours. This explains why young as well as old women were accused, not to mention a significant minority of men. Take two men called Godfrey (no relation). In 1617, William Godfrey, an integrated yeoman farmer in Kent, was accused of *maleficia* from leaving ghosts in a house to murdering children. In colonial Massachusetts, John Godfrey was tried repeatedly for using a spirit to attack neighbours. Evidently people could think about witches in two different ways simultaneously, one shaped by information, the other by feeling. Stereotypes influenced opinion but didn't restrict its expression. Actions usually spoke louder than words. Evans-Pritchard noticed how Azande beliefs were actualized not intellectualized: 'their tenets are expressed in socially controlled behaviour rather than in doctrines'.

The tightest control on behaviour came from the administration of justice, not just preventing and punishing crime, but obliging communities to deal with crime in officially sanctioned ways.

Only by instilling this habit – law over custom – would the early modern state extend its power to the periphery. All sorts of malefactors got reported; but how did you catch a witch, and how were you supposed to proceed beyond pouring your heart out to a magistrate? This is where tests came in, methods of diagnosis and identification that typically were unofficial, collective, and legally dubious. In parts of Africa, the traditional procedure is to feed poison to domestic fowls to see how they react. In Europe, water in a pail was expected to shimmer when a witch walked past; a sieve suspended from shears would rotate when her name was spoken. Thatch from a suspect's roof might be burned to smoke her out, and boiling a patient's urine was meant to cause a witch pain; it could even burst her bladder. Witches were made to recite the Lord's Prayer. And they were weighed, sometimes against bibles; the Dutch town of Oudewater built giant scales. If a death was attributed to witchcraft, suspects might be required to touch the corpse to see if fresh blood appeared – a providential sign of guilt.

Recourse to a professional could help. Classical soothsayers, Dark Age shamans, African witch-doctors, and early modern cunning folk all performed the same function: to reify unspoken suspicions, turning private thoughts into public actions. In England, midwives and 'juries of matrons' searched the bodies of the accused looking for teats where diabolic familiars or imps were supposed to suckle. Then there were self-appointed witchfinders. Some, like the female *chirurgiennes* of Franche-Comté, would prick for insensible areas of flesh – the Devil's marks; others, like the English 'witchfinder general' Matthew Hopkins, led interrogations and encouraged witnesses to take their complaints to law. On occasion, Hopkins oversaw swimming tests, the so-called 'ordeal by water', which held that a witch would be rejected by the pure element in a symbolic reversal of baptism.

In his treatise on witches *Daemonologie* (1597), James VI of Scotland (soon to be king of England too) had approved 'fleeting

8. An English witch is subjected to the water ordeal, 1613

upon the water', although it had no status in law and was widely
seen as sacrilegious. Across Europe, ordeals had been banned in
the 13th century, but their importance for rural decision-making
meant they lingered on. And with the rise of witch-trials in the
mid-16th century, so the swimming test (and other ordeals)
became even more prominent. Practice was uneven. In 1595,
Philip II outlawed the water ordeal in the Spanish Netherlands,
and a few years later so did the French *Parlement* and the bishop
of Bremen. By contrast, magistrates in Münster and Osnabrück
sanctioned it, as did some English justices in the 1640s. By this
time, however, most governors knew that whatever value these
rituals had as reassuring communal theatre, they offended God
and threatened public order. Witchfinders still operate in the
developing world, mostly in more lawless states and regions such
as India's Bihar province where '*ojahs*' sniff out witches so they
can be killed.

Brickbats and broomsticks

When one version of the truth trumps another, the consequences can be liberating or lethal. An *ojah*'s victims might know they are innocent, but what use is that if the political consensus disagrees? There's comfort in the discoveries of science's founding fathers – Copernicus, Galileo, Kepler, Newton – in that they appear to have led us from intolerance and superstition into a world of rationalism and progress. Seen in the round, however, their lives testify to the inertia of established wisdom and the difficulty of achieving what historians of science call a 'paradigm shift': a slow and halting transition from one way of seeing things to another. Galileo was forced to abjure by the Inquisition, so heretical were his theories; and Newton the scientist was also Newton the magus. But it is Johannes Kepler's story that most intrigues. My biographical dictionary has plenty to say about his studies at Tübingen and Gras in the 1590s, and his time as court astronomer to Rudolf II, patron and persecutor of John Dee. There are details of his books and planetary laws, building on Copernican cosmology, and of his suggestion that mathematics was the language of God. But there's no mention of his mother's trial for witchcraft.

Katharina Kepler lived with her husband, an innkeeper, at Leonberg in the duchy of Württemberg. Around 1615, she fell out with neighbours the Reinbolds, who subsequently accused her of bewitching their children. A counter-suit for slander caused the Reinbolds to seek legal and medical advice, and by 1619 Katharina was under investigation. Meanwhile, her son was unable to help because of his dissidence from the Lutheran orthodoxy in Württemberg. In 1620, Katharina was imprisoned, but refused to confess even when shown the instruments of torture. In the end, she was released, but her incarceration had taken its toll and she died soon after. As for Kepler, clearly he had inherited his mother's independence of mind, a quality which led to suspicions that he was both a closet Calvinist and an ally of the Jesuits, as well as enabling him in 1619 to produce a sublime Neoplatonic interpretation of the universe, dedicated to James I of England. Katharina Kepler may not have been a witch, but her son's mysticism was very real and, as with Newton, it was inseparable from his empiricism.

The process for investigating Kepler's mother was painstaking, involving some important men in the duchy. This was not unusual in the 17th century: witchcraft and justice were serious matters. Katharina's case was considered by lawyers at the University of Tübingen and her release ordered by the duke himself. In the 16th century, the quest for truth about witchcraft in general, and about specific cases, had gradually converged. Even Heinrich Kramer had realized the persuasiveness of mixing theology and legal experience, and subsequent books used a similar method, for example papal judge Paulus Grillandus's *Tractatus de Hereticis et Sortligiis* ('Treatise on Heretics and Witches') of 1524. Most printed works after 1550 were guides to jurists and interrogators. These included several re-editions of the *Malleus Maleficarum*, as well as Jean Bodin's *De la Démonomanie des Sorciers* ('On the Demon-Mania of Witches') in 1580, translated into German by the humanist Johann Fischart. Studies by French judges Nicolas Rémy (1595), Henri Boguet (1602), and Pierre de Lancre (1612) built on the existing literature – especially Bodin – with their own anecdotes thrown in. Not that any of this led to consensus: far from it, in fact.

The witch-hunt did not follow a simple trajectory between credulity and scepticism. At its beginning and its end, debate raged as to whether witchcraft was both real *and* demonstrable. Sometimes the argument swung to the affirmative, sometimes the negative. Jean Bodin, author of the *Démonomanie*, believed that if he established the reality of witchcraft as a crime, then individual cases would not need to be proved in court with the certainty required for other offences. Witchcraft was *crimen exceptum* – an exceptional crime. This might sound feeble-minded, but Bodin was one of Europe's finest thinkers: a jurist, theologian, historian, and natural philosopher – a true Renaissance man. To him, the integrity of the godly state was supremely important, witches its biggest threat. They could be fought, he argued, by accumulating expertise among judges and academics. Against a background of tension between Catholics and Protestants in France, Bodin advocated toleration; but this was no human rights issue. Rather, he insisted, Christians had to unite to resist the forces of Satan massing on the horizon.

Bodin's intellectual enemy was Johann Weyer, who in some respects resembled him. A direct contemporary, Weyer was a physician to the duke of Cleves, well versed in philosophy and law, and a former apprentice to the Renaissance magus Agrippa von Nettesheim. Weyer's faith is unclear. The fact that he has been linked to Erasmian, Lutheran, and (less plausibly) Catholic persuasions indicates his latitudinarian thinking as well as how misleading such labels can be. In 1563, he published *De Praestigiis Daemonum* ('On the Illusions of Demons'), which ran to several editions, including translations and a populist abridged version. Sigmund Freud included it in his top ten books, calling Weyer the father of modern psychiatry. But Freud had taken what he liked about Weyer and left the rest – the same habit that overlooks Newton's alchemy and Kepler's mysticism. In fact, Weyer's thinking was much closer to Bodin and even to Kramer. He argued that the Devil was *more* powerful than was supposed, obviating the need for witches; the accused were deluded victims. Like the legal demonologists, Weyer amassed information about witches but reversed the logical inference.

There was nothing polite about debating core truths of the universe: contributions were brickbats hurled at opponents. James I reviled Weyer, as did many advocates of witch-hunting. He was even called a *sagarum patronus*, or defender of witches. Yet he had supporters. In England, Reginald Scot, who had read Kramer, Bodin, and Weyer, was outspoken in his scepticism. Though not a lawyer, he had attended witch-trials and been appalled. His

Discoverie of Witchcraft (1584) was condemned by every major English demonologist, and according to legend King James had it burned by the hangman. Like Weyer, however, Scot was no harbinger of the Enlightenment. His main preoccupation was the denial of providence implied by witch-beliefs – failure to accept misfortune as judgement – and their consonance with Catholic superstition. Neither did Scot reject demonic agency, a step on the slippery slope towards atheism. Scot's religion is as hard to determine as Weyer's, and it is understandable why historians have linked both men to the Family of Love, a clandestine mystical sect.

On the ground, the picture was confused. A severe witch-hunt in the duchy of Bavaria in 1590 created an almost paradoxical situation in which governors and governed alike were primed for further purging, while being extremely wary about excessive persecution and injustice. Protestants in neighbouring states scorned Bavarian credulity regarding evidence, and even within Catholic Bavaria two 'parties' evolved, one for witch-hunting, the other against. By 1630, the moderates had prevailed, but now zealous Protestants had become more willing to accept more dubious forms of physical evidence. The two sides in the Reformation, each with diverse opinions in its own camp, effectively swapped positions within the space of forty years.

While philosophical scepticism remained a minority position, legal scepticism was widespread. Contrary to the 'black legend' of sadistic intolerance the Spanish Inquisition was progressive in its thinking. Witchcraft was hard to prove, so early in the 17th century inquisitors stopped trying. The same happened in the Netherlands, and but for the revolution of the 1640s England might have followed suit. For all James I's worrying about witchcraft in Scotland – he had been horrified when a witch he was examining told him snippets of pillow-talk from his honeymoon – from 1603 as king of England he was much more sceptical. As with his contemporaries, the monarch's ideas were political as well as philosophical. By 1600, the English Reformation was no longer just a war between Catholics and Protestants, but between radical Protestants (puritans) and their orthodox counterparts. James aimed to deflate puritan sails, while continuing to suppress Catholicism.

Exorcism was a key area for puritans and Jesuits to make rival claims to unique dispensation of divine power. Expose demoniacs as hysterics and frauds and the legitimacy of both sets of extremists would be undermined. So James did just this, taking a personal interest in 'possessed' teenagers, who were doubtless astonished and terrified to find themselves being interviewed by the king. When a witch-hunt broke out in Lancashire in 1634, Charles I, James's son, ordered his physician William Harvey to examine the accused. Harvey, celebrated discoverer of the circulation of blood, found no evidence of guilt but neither did he rule out that possibility. Scepticism grew *within* the accepted world of demons, rather than *outside* in stark opposition.

The debate intensified in the 1650s and sceptics gained ground. The paradigm was shifting. Scot's *Discoverie* was republished with a title page suggesting that 'witches' should be treated with food and medicine, echoing Weyer's idea that they were infirm. (One 16th-century Swiss physician had even suggested that suspects would benefit from music, dancing, and sex.) In England, controversy centred on two scions of the same intellectual stock, with contrasting visions of nature. Joseph Glanvill was an anti-materialist Anglican clergyman, John Webster a doctor who questioned the validity of testimony. Webster didn't doubt the existence of demons, but argued that they worked inside minds not through transmutation into God's creatures. Glanvill and Webster locked horns in print. An early version of Glanvill's defence of spirits, *Saducismus Triumphatus* (1681), appeared in 1666, marketed at a wide audience. Diarist Samuel Pepys judged it 'well written but not very convincing'. Yet Pepys, like many urbane gentlemen, was gripped: he read the third edition on Christmas Day 1667.

Print extended informed debate into the coffee-houses of Restoration London. Readers were either persuaded by Glanvill's take on witchcraft or they were not. Pepys seems more like us than Glanvill, yet social and intellectual differences between them were slight. Opinion was only narrowly determined by ideas; broadly it was a matter of culture. Men like Pepys rejected witch-beliefs as a fashionable reflex, personal conviction aside. Seven centuries earlier, the *Canon Episcopi* had doubted that witches rode out into the night because it was theologically untenable; now such notions were rejected because they were silly. At the trial of Jane Wenham (1712), the last English woman convicted of *maleficium*, the judge responded to the charge that she flew on a broomstick by joking that there was no law against flying. Through such mockery, a self-fashioning, self-conscious European middle class distanced itself from the superstitious masses.

We shouldn't forget, however, that Jane Wenham *was* convicted, even if the conviction was swiftly overturned. This late in the day, the truth of witchcraft was still poised between belief and doubt – the recurring tension between faith and curiosity mentioned in Chapter 1. For a relatively short period of time, between the 15th and 18th centuries, witchcraft was made real, not just through superstition and primitivism but through law and science. Ironically, law and science would also be the means by which the idea was exploded in public life.

Chapter 5
Justice

Custom and courts

I'm looking up at research files on a high shelf, the faded spines
hard to read. Leafing through a couple takes me back twenty years,
when I first walked into an archive looking for witches. In the
Public Record Office, I pored over the depositions of the northern
assizes and rummaged in boxes of grubby papers from the
palatinate of Lancaster. At Canterbury Cathedral, I waded through
the records of the Elizabethan church courts, great leather-bound
books full of crabbed entries. At first, they seemed illegible. But
with patience the dead words came back to life, and a strange
world lifted off the page.

The Lancaster papers were uncatalogued, so you never knew what
you'd find next. My notes tell of forgery and theft, slander and
sedition, assault and homicide. Witches, too, came to light.
A woman's testimony from 1665 alleged that a witch gave her
husband back-pain 'as though he had been pricked by an awl'.
In 1681, Mary Ashworth and her son were accused of murdering
Janet Hoyle who had been nipped and squashed, and nightly saw
apparitions of the witches. In another case, a suspect confessed
that a friend had killed calves 'with two little spirits'. The
Canterbury records were in better order, but no less full of
surprises. Among presentments for brawling and fornicating and

skipping church, there were villagers reported for magical practices such as healing and divination. I even found cases of *maleficium*: a nurse said to have killed a child; a murderous prayer; beggars avenging neighbourly meanness. In 1560, James Sloman fell out with Robert Brayne while they were working together, and the next day lost his best cow. To some extent, such cases confirm the Thomas–Macfarlane thesis; but the relationships and conflicts go beyond 'charity-refused'. One man suffered after Brayne's wife refused to lend *him* a horse. And the feuds were not between individuals but households.

We should ask what these records *don't* tell us, as well as what they do. Pessimists say there can be no history of popular culture, only of its suppression. In Chapter 3, we saw how Elizabeth Mortlock became a witch when her life was refracted through the prism of officialdom; we know about her healing only because she was censured for it. Witchcraft was relative, indeed correlative with the communities and courts that condemned it. Unlike novelists, historians are only as good as their archives, and many historians of witchcraft rely on legal records to resurrect historical reality. There is a curious parallel here with the work of inquisitors and magistrates. Witchcraft was not a crime that spoke for itself like stealing or fighting, a deed that happened openly and visibly. To punish it, it had to be laboriously extracted from its social setting and dressed as evidence. So witchcraft testimony is doubly decontextualized, first by early modern courts looking for signs of demonic malice, then again by scholars with research agendas, selecting records, making notes, constructing arguments.

Legal and historical truths about witchcraft were – and are – shaped in a triangular matrix of governors, governed, and those who study them. This began with the desire to criminalize folk religion, of which there are many ancient examples. Roman proscription of *veneficium* in the 2nd century BC has already been mentioned, likewise the legal code of AD 297. But in the 4th and 5th centuries, when Christianity was established, more measures were introduced. Emperor Valentinian I made *maleficium* a capital offence, and Theodosius II forbade all forms of magic, however benign they seemed to his subjects. This departed from previous imperial policy, which had been clear about the illegality of harmful magic, less so the popular sorcery. A decree of AD 389 ordered anyone even aware of witchery to report it. In the 6th century, Augustine's maxim that magicians consorted with demons became the basis of all laws and edicts thereafter.

The early church did not execute witches, seeing their offence as reformable. Only in the Middle Ages did the campaign against heresy intensify, the legislative apex being Pope Innocent's bull, *Summis desiderantes affectibus* (1484), on which Heinrich Kramer built his claim to authority. Even then, reliance on secular power to kill diabolists was considerable, an arrangement lasting into the Reformation era. The Holy Roman Empire's *Carolina* code (1532) explicitly forbade witchcraft, and in 1542 the first Witchcraft Act was introduced in England. Cases of witchcraft at the Canterbury church courts peter out in the 1570s as the assizes assumed responsibility to try them according to statute.

Passing laws was easy, implementing them less so. In their internal affairs, pre-modern states were weak. They were often unstable and had to extend governance over vast territories; professional bureaucracies were, at best, nascent; the efficiency of tax collection varied; there were no police forces in the modern sense, and few nations had standing armies. Instead states depended on, first, ideology communicated in words, symbols, and rituals; and second, the authority of local governors derived from land-based social ties. The success of state formation, energetically advanced after 1500, therefore hinged on strained and ambiguous relationships between centre and periphery, mixing consent where possible, coercion where necessary, and plenty of compromise. As we saw in Chapter 2, the Roman Empire and the medieval church had difficulty enforcing anti-magical laws. This was true even regarding *maleficium*, the heinousness of which was consensual.

The problem was not that people didn't want black witches to be punished, only that they wanted to do it themselves according to custom. Sociologists might see this as tension between the parochial habits of *Gemeinschaft* (community) and the greater unifying claims of *Gesellschaft* (society).

Traditionally, European justice was dispensed locally, with the onus on the individual to prove his case – that is, 'accusatory' justice. Ordeals were key. Often this involved a suspect holding a red-hot iron, binding the wound, and reaching a verdict by how long it took to heal. The ordeal invoked divine will to discover what man alone could not. For this reason, in 1215 ordeals were forbidden as presumptuous tests of God. Instead, Roman law inquisitions assumed responsibility for determining truth, in retrospect a shift from superstition to science, if not yet a paradigm shift. Here we see growing confidence that humans might grasp the hidden and the sublime, providentially guided but without miraculous intervention. By custom, the *lex talionis* dictated that the accuser would be punished if an ordeal went against him: a powerful deterrent. Many preferred rough justice: the knock on the head, the knife in the guts – solutions at odds with the monopoly of violence desired by state-builders. By 1300, however, although the burden of proof usually remained with accusers, crimes could be reported with relative impunity to the authorities, who might also investigate.

The weakness of the centre inhibited a complete shift from accusation to inquisition. Hungary retained its accusatory justice, as did England, where the onus stayed with plaintiffs and magistrates were local amateurs. But even there ordeals were replaced with juries, agents of human decision-making. (Scotland had a hybrid system of inquisitions and juries.) In practice, law officers everywhere relied upon information provided by ordinary witnesses. By 1400, the fiction that English juries were 'self-informing' had been abandoned, and use of testimony made routine. Despite reassurances that unsuccessful plaintiffs would not be punished, some risk (e.g. shame or counter-suit for defamation) remained. So community backing was important, and people clung to swimming and other ordeals to substantiate claims and bolster confidence. The need was accentuated by the fact that secular inquisitorial justice required better proof, which typically was lacking for witchcraft. This explains why it was treated as *crimen exceptum*. After 1500, witch-trials were easier for people to initiate, but harder for them to end to their satisfaction.

'Witch-craze'

Dan Brown's thriller *The Da Vinci Code* states that during the witch-craze, 'the church burned at the stake an astounding five million women'. Astounding indeed, but untrue. Granted, this is not a reliable source (nor a great novel), but tens of millions of people have read it. So Brown has helped to perpetuate a widespread myth about the scale and cause of the witch-hunt. Occasionally you see even higher figures. Radical feminists and neo-pagans have claimed that *nine* million perished during what they call 'the burning times'. There's no substance to this. The origin of 'nine million' is an elementary multiplication error made by an 18th-century German antiquary, enshrined as fact by a Viennese professor a century later. Historians depend on other historians' books as well as on archives, and readers believe what they want.

Another problem is fakery. In 1972, historians at the University of Pennsylvania edited a collection of witchcraft documents, one of which pointed to the mid-14th-century origins of witch-hunting in southern France. Three years later, Norman Cohn, an expert on the history of witchcraft, revealed that this story had been invented, embellished, and repeated uncritically for centuries. (In America, Richard Kieckhefer reached the same conclusion around the same time.) The Pennsylvanians had taken their lead in good faith from early 20th-century historian Joseph Hansen; Hansen's source was Étienne Léon de Lamothe-Langon's *Histoire de l'Inquisition* (1829); and Lamothe-Langon, the villain of the piece, had concocted his account using an 18th-century work, which itself exploited a 15th-century chronicle that may or may not have been a 16th-century hoax. As a result, it was widely accepted that in the 1330s Toulousian inquisitors had fashioned a new stereotype from Catharism, diabolism, and *maleficium*: a sect of antisocial, devil-worshipping witches to be exterminated. Subsequent editions of the documents acknowledged the error, but the contamination had already spread. The old version remains on shelves in libraries around the world.

Cohn was hard on Lamothe-Langon, but more forgiving to Hansen who was gulled by the 'simplicity of his heart'. Hansen, an archivist in Cologne, published an influential book which, apart from broadcasting a medieval myth, demonstrated the value of returning to the records of criminal trials. In the decades before the Second World War, this idea inspired historians like Cecil L'Estrange Ewen, who found an extraordinary quantity of witchcraft cases in English archives, including almost every indictment surviving for the south-eastern assizes between 1560 and 1701 – all 790 of them. In many places Alan Macfarlane and Keith Thomas searched for witch-trials, they found Ewen had been there first. Today all historians of witchcraft are indebted to Ewen, and to Hansen (killed in an air-raid in 1943). Most have their own archival patch: Macfarlane in Essex; Carlo Ginzburg in Friuli; Robin Briggs in Lorraine. German historians often have their own city to work on. Thanks to Hansen and Ewen, I ended up in the Kent archives, drawing red dots on maps, and later in the record offices of East Anglia.

Ewen's work demonstrated, among other things, that there were surprisingly few witch-trials in England, perhaps no more than 1,000 in the early modern period, only half of which resulted in executions. Archival research across Europe also produced downward estimates and differing timescales. The witch-hunt proper hadn't started in the 14th century, nor in the 15th, but in the

9. The Devil abandons German witches to the executioner's fire, an illustration from a printed broadside, 1555

later 16th century; some countries had ended their trials in the early 17th century, others didn't get going until much later. Chronologically, spatially, and statistically, there was little consistency. If by 'witch-craze', we mean a coherent, coordinated pan-European campaign, it wasn't really a witch-craze at all. It was patchy, fragmented, unfocused, even random.

The worst decades were the 1590s, 1630s, and 1660s. Some of the most intense panics (which we'll explore in the next chapter) happened in southern Germany; but Italy and Spain, heartland of the Catholic Inquisition, had few trials and peaked around 1550. Even within Germany the picture was uneven. The Holy Roman Empire, a central European patchwork of states, is often held up as the cradle of the witch-craze, when many regions saw little or no persecution. Cologne and Westphalia experienced savage bursts, and the situation was appalling in the prince-bishopric of Würzburg; the bishopric of Münster, however, was largely unaffected. In Bamberg's grimmest decade (1623–33), there were over 600 executions; a few miles away, by contrast, Rothenburg saw only a handful of witchcraft cases between 1549 and 1709, involving just 65 suspects. Excluding Normandy and Lorraine, in France persecution was modest. In Spain, as in the Netherlands, it was pretty much all over by 1610. Swedish trials took off in the 1660s; in Poland, the time-frame was 1675–1720; and Hungary's key decade was the 1720s. Variegation of the map doesn't seem particularly tied to religion: Orthodox Russia, Catholic Ireland, and Protestant Holland all had low levels of prosecution; some of the worst outbreaks relative to population happened in Calvinist Scotland – that is, eastern, lowland Scotland – and a number of German Catholic states. In England, the county of Essex suffered most, and nationally the bulk of the trials occurred in the late 16th and mid-17th centuries.

By the 1980s, the sizes, timings, types, and causes of witch-trials still seemed connected, but more within each example than between them. Differences began to outweigh similarities, old models crumbled, and the idea that the witch-hunt was an orchestrated purge by clerical elites laid to rest. A symposium in Stockholm in 1984 led to a collection of essays edited by Bengt Ankarloo and Gustav Henningsen. Here were studies of witch-trials not just in England, France, and Germany – cradle of the Reformation and traditional focus for the witch-hunt – but in Hungary, Estonia, Finland, Denmark, Portugal, Norway – even Iceland. In the early 1990s, another conference and more essays continued the search for origins and outcomes: now everywhere seemed special, and instead of models we had 'many reasons why'.

The only obvious way to reunite the data was to add up statistics. Just how many people had been tried as witches? Historians knew nine million was too high, but archival research brought them closer to the real figure. For much of the 20th century, it was believed that Scotland had executed around 7,500 witches, a figure suggested by H. C. Lea, an American historian inspired by Hansen: now this came down to 1,500. Poland's toll, calculated in the 1950s, was 15,000; less than one-fifth of that is probably nearer the mark.

Numbers everywhere had been exaggerated. Today combined estimates for Europe, Scandinavia, and America vary between 90,000 and 100,000 trials in the period 1400 to 1800. The worst time overall was 1560 to 1630. Perhaps half the prosecutions took place in German territories, several thousand in Baden Württemberg alone. A sizeable proportion occurred in neighbouring states, especially Switzerland, where perhaps 10,000 people were tried. In the borderlands of Lorraine, there were 5,000 trials, although in the vastly larger kingdom of France, just 3,000. Scandinavia also had around 3,000 trials, as did the British Isles. Spain and Italy accounted for 10,000; Eastern Europe and Russia half that.

The accuracy of these numbers matters, just as it matters for the millions who died in 20th-century genocides. To respect the dead, you have to tell the truth about them. And unless witch-hunts are precisely quantified, they cannot be precisely explained. As Emmanuel Le Roy Ladurie once wrote: 'of what use is an incorrect million for proving a correct idea?' Statistical errors had long been bound up with chronology and causation, principally the medieval and clerical character of the 'witch-craze'; now that came to an end. From the ruins of Lamothe-Langon's fictions and various flimsy post-Enlightenment assumptions, a sturdier structure was raised by empirical historians. Like science, history has its paradigm shifts, and for witchcraft this was it.

Let's look in more detail at what had really happened. First of all, medieval ecclesiastical courts, like their Reformation counterparts, prosecuted sorcerers and magicians. In 1465, a man was hauled before the bishop's court in Cambridge charged with possessing writings on the black art, inscribed metal plates, and a gilded wand. He said he had bought them for four marks, believing they would earn him an abundance of gold and silver. But this trial was a bit of routine administration, not part of a concerted drive against witches; indeed, although the magician's offence would have been seen as a diabolic delusion, this didn't make him a devil-worshipping rebel – the stereotype that was to emerge. There were many such impious fools.

Medieval witchcraft trials could be more explicit and serious, as we saw with Alice Kyteler in the 1320s. A century after that episode, England burned the mystical warrior Joan of Arc for heresy and treason, but with supplementary charges of invoking spirits. A few years later, Eleanor Cobham, duchess of Gloucester, did penance for attempting to kill Henry VI using sorcery; her accomplices, an astrologer and cunning woman, were executed. But these were political show trials, side effects of the transition of power from medieval courts to modern governments. This was only a vague precursor of the practice whereby villagers pursued malevolent neighbours at law. That came in the 16th century with demographic growth, economic competition, cultural fragmentation, confessional state-building, and the expansion of the law – a far more extensive transformation of European life. Even then, as Brian Levack has pointed out, 'witch-hunts did not start spontaneously in those communities that were intellectually, legally and psychologically prepared to experience them'. The assumption that they did explains the German antiquary's mistake that took so long to correct.

Only in the 16th century did ideology coincide with social necessity and political opportunity. In theology, law, and the popular imagination, the witch came to life as universal enemy. 'The most notorious traitor and rebel that can be is the witch', declared English puritan William Perkins, 'for she renounceth God himself, the king of kings, she leaves the society of his church and people, she bindeth herself in league with the Devil'; it's hard to imagine an educated man putting it like that in 1500 or 1700. The stories of Reformation and witch-hunt are elaborately intertwined. Protestant reformers, who had unmasked the Pope as Antichrist, sensed the imminence of the Apocalypse: an enraged Satan's final battle with Christ. Emphasis shifted from the 'seven deadly sins' to the Ten Commandments, including a ban on worshipping false idols. Mosaic law also provided the crucial text: Exodus 22:18 – 'thou shalt not suffer a witch to live'. As the Bible moved to the centre of religious culture, so its injunctions against idolatry and sorcery entered legal codes and mentalities. In the same way that model Protestants covenanted with Christ, the most heinous sinners made covenants with Satan. Framed as law, this idea allowed Christians to fight the Devil in court as well as from the pulpit.

The competence of temporal courts was vital; even Joan of Arc was burned by the state not the church. Thanks to archival studies since the 1970s, it is clear that the 'witch-craze' was essentially a secular legal phenomenon. There are some interesting patterns. Peak periods of witch-hunting correspond with war, plague, and harvest failure, though not necessarily at exactly the same time. South-west Germany in the 1630s, where these conditions were present, experienced a temporary dip in prosecutions. In 1635–44, Franche-Comté saw relatively few trials, even though the region was ravaged by war; and in the same years England, despite profound economic and political uncertainty, barely any. England and Franche-Comté had their witch-hunts in the end, yet both indicate that when the courts couldn't or wouldn't try witches – in wartime often because of administrative failure – the problem appeared to contract. I say *appeared* to contract because people's fear and anger may well have increased, but went undocumented.

Above all, we now know that witch-trials were rarer than was once supposed. Examining the evidence in detail place by place, year by year, we see differences great and small, but nearly always get the impression that prosecuting witches was an unusual way to resist them. Isolated from their social contexts, the legal documents that have revealed so much are silent about the millions of suspicions, accusations, assaults, and lynchings that never reached the courts. The witch-hunt may have been mainly a judicial phenomenon; but we should remember that it wasn't *only* a judicial phenomenon.

Pain and fire

The gallery of images that makes up popular knowledge of the witch-hunt is incomplete without the torture chamber: a dungeon full of baroque contraptions for inflicting pain. This picture was refined in waves of Protestant propaganda where it illustrated perfectly the cruelty of Catholic Inquisitions. More recently, horror films and attractions such as London Dungeon have kept this ghastly scenario alive in popular culture, barely vitiated by the celebrated Monty Python sketch.

Torture is so abhorrent to civilized people that there's a danger of misunderstanding its history. In March 2009, British newspapers reported how a suspected terrorist was subjected to 'medieval torture' in Morocco with the connivance of the secret service. The moral repugnance of this is plain, but in history things are rarely that simple. Torture calls for an 'emic' interpretation, a relativistic approach. This may offend. But as with rejecting evil as historical explanation, and insisting on precise statistics, to understand is not the same as to condone. Good historians neither condemn nor make excuses for their subjects: readers can do that for themselves.

Like propaganda, gruesome dramas and museum tableaux omit the context necessary to appreciate what was going on. Voyeurs of suffering may not care; but it matters what torturers actually did, and thought they were doing, to understand why such practices were institutionalized. Today, although torture may be widespread, at least its secrecy indicates that it is politically taboo, a *prima facie* breach of human rights. One of the hardest things to explain to students is why the use of torture – 'getting medieval', to quote Tarantino's *Pulp Fiction* – was once a progressive technique to prevent miscarriages of justice. In some ways, torture belongs to the modern rather than medieval era in that it reflected optimism that truth, untainted by malice, might be discovered without recourse to superstition. Torture was an important part of Roman-canonical inquisitorial procedure, an innovation to banish ordeals and local customs in criminal suits. Justice, like science and history, could be empirical.

Torture was arranged in grades of severity. Operatives were meant to be skilled because they obeyed inquisitors seeking truth without causing unnecessary suffering. The mildest form was the *territio* – merely showing a suspect the instruments of torture. In 1657, Tereshka Malakurov and his wife Olenka were questioned about witchcraft in the Russian town of Lukh, 'in the torture chamber, in sight of the instruments of torture'; the *territio* was also used on Kepler's mother. In both cases, the accused continued to deny the charges; but this might not have been seen as obstinacy, rather as good evidence given the solemnity under which it was extracted. In Rothenburg ob der Tauber, torture was used on *accusers* to ensure their honesty and to deter malicious time-wasters. Many states felt accusatory justice to be obsolete because it encouraged neighbourhood conspiracies while invoking divine adjudication.

Humans are fascinated by horror and suffering; perhaps at some deep psychological level, torture dares us to peek at hell on earth. Several European cities now have museums of torture into which tourists can wander. There they see things seen by Tereshka Malakurov and Katharina Kepler. A common torture was the *strappado*, hoisting by the arms tied behind the suspect's back; when weights were added, this was 'squassation'. Other devices included thumbscrews, leg-clamps, heated iron frames, the rack, and the 'iron maiden' (a spike-lined sarcophagus), all extensively used. Accused repeatedly by the people of Lukh, Malakurov endured increasingly severe tortures, including the application of red-hot pincers, until he confessed. Nor was harm inflicted always temporary. It was said of Dr Fian, a Scots suspect in the 1590s, that 'his legs were crushed and beaten together as small as might be, and the bones and flesh so bruised that the blood and marrow spouted forth in great abundance'.

10. A French witch is tortured by the Inquisition using 'squassation', that is, the *strappado* with weights attached

For all its academic formality, torture was frequently unregulated and botched. Witch-crazes stemmed from legally dubious denunciations made under duress. In regions far from central government, and in independent jurisdictions, abuse was rife. The Bamberg 'witch-house' built by Bishop Johann Georg II, with its own cells, is a case in point. Dragged to the stake in 1590, a convicted witch at Werdenfels in Bavaria called to the crowd: 'You pious women, fly across the mountains; for whoever falls into the hands of the torturer must die!'. In 1652, allegations by Scottish prisoners that they had been hanged by the thumbs and burned with candles prompted an investigation by English judges. Sleep deprivation (the *tormentum insomniae*) was also common in Scotland because it was effective and did not cause visible injury. The English used torture only in special criminal cases, not due to superior humanitarianism but because torture was superfluous when so much trust was placed in juries. Ironically, this meant people used force unofficially, as in 1603 when the servants of two Norfolk gentlemen flashed gunpowder in a woman's face and threatened to burn her unless she confessed. In East Anglian communities, illegal sleep deprivation was a widely used pre-trial procedure in the wild years of the mid-1640s.

Ultimately, torture, whether state-sanctioned or irregular, did not solve the essential problem of witchcraft as an offence: how to discover and prove it. What to do with those who *were* found guilty caused less soul-searching. St Augustine had recommended that all magicians, as *de facto* diabolists, be put to death, and after 1500, in cases where diabolism was detected, relatively few disagreed. Medieval heretics were burned on pyres, obliterated from society, and it followed that witches should be punished similarly. The *Canon Episcopi* did not demand execution, mainly because it disputed witches' fantastic claims, and in keeping with that most culprits chastised by the church were spared. More was to be gained by exhibiting them as penitents – the fate of the alleged plotter Eleanor Cobham and the healer Elizabeth Mortlock. Our 15th-century Cambridge magician had his kit confiscated, and was made to fast; his book was burned, but he was not.

With growing secular responsibility, however, came increased use of the death penalty. In rare instances when the early church did condemn magicians as heretics, it handed them to state officials for execution, as with Joan of Arc. Some witches were imprisoned (often a death sentence in itself), flogged, or mutilated. But the most common punishment was capital. Inquisitorial jurisdictions, including that in Scotland, burned witches, usually after garrotting them. The French hanged witches first; in Germany occasionally they were beheaded. English witches were felons according to common law and so were choked to death at the end of a rope; a witch might be burned if she bewitched her husband – the crime of petty treason – but this seldom happened. Colonial America copied English practice. Some countries drowned witches, or buried them alive – the fate of Olenka Malakurov. Executions were spectacular public theatres of pain and punishment, admonition and purification, where heinous malefactors were conveyed to heaven for judgement and spectators might mend their own ways.

Witches in real-life accounts, spread by word of mouth and print, were usually already dead; most news reports originated in the hubbub of an execution. For clergymen and law enforcers, this lent witchcraft stories a narrative structure where wickedness led inexorably to justice. Villagers hearing these tales may have been emboldened to use the law against witches and to steer clear from temptation lest they fall into committing the ultimate crime. But what was the legal reality? People were just as liable to believe myths about witchcraft as they are today; it's that kind of subject: alarming and beguiling. And remember that many early modern Europeans had no first-hand experience of a witch-trial. Their knowledge was based on rumour and sermons and news-sheets, information that was selective, redacted, embroidered, and garbled.

With more accurate numbers of trials has come a better idea of execution rates. They are surprisingly low, given this was supposed to be a craze. In many European regions, the proportion executed was about half the number of trials – as Ewen found for England. This means somewhere between 40,000 and 50,000. In exceptional cases, such as in the Pays de Vaud, the execution rate was 90%; in Luxembourg and Scotland, it approached 80%. There were over 20,000 German executions, suggesting the typical rate of 50%. But in Geneva and south-eastern England, it was less than 25%. In Finland, only 16% of prosecuted witches died. In France, the *Parlement* in Paris operated a rigorous appeals procedure, reviewing over 1,000 convictions between 1565 and 1640, frequently in favour of the accused. Spain's largest witch-hunt involved a staggering 1,900 suspects, of whom just eleven were condemned. Rothenburg ob der Tauber, meanwhile, executed three witches in its entire history.

Chapter 6
Rage

Panic

In the archives of Munich's municipal library there is a remarkable letter. It was written in August 1629 by the chancellor to Philipp Adolf von Ehrenberg, prince-bishop of Würzburg. Twelve years earlier, under the reformist bishop Julius Echter von Mespelbrunn, over 300 witches had been burned in 11 months – an event many had hoped would never reoccur. The letter, written to a friend, describes how it did.

> Ah, the woe and misery of it – there are still four hundred in this city, high and low, of every rank and sex, nay, even clerics, so strongly accused that they may be arrested at any hour.

This was a witch-panic: no one was above suspicion. Between 1626 and 1631, Würzburg executed another 900 people, affecting every part of local society.

Suspicions grew into accusations, accusations into trials, which, in turn, generated more accusations and trials. Tales of bewitchment became irrelevant, overtaken by unsubstantiated charges of diabolism, usually made by tortured suspects. In time, the vicious circle would be broken, but not before dozens – or, as in Würzburg, hundreds – had lost their lives. Contemporaries described forests of blackened stakes, a hellish scene straight from the popular gallery of 'witch-craze' images. There is no shortage of examples. Sustained panics in Alpine Italy and Switzerland, 1428–36, and in Dauphiné in France, 1420–50, each resulted in 500 executions; in the duchy of Milan, 2,000 died between 1480 and 1520. The bloodiest witch-hunts, however, occurred during the Reformation, c. 1580–1680. Independent jurisdictions, common in the German territories, were the most affected. Trier, Nassau, Ellwangen, and Mergentheim, all small Catholic states, each put to death 350–450 witch suspects, mostly in quite short periods. Like Würzburg, the bishopric of Bamberg dispatched several hundred, 1616–30; the authorities in Cologne and Mecklenburg, 2,000 a piece. A single smouldering accusation could become a conflagration. At Rouen in 1670, the interrogation of 9 suspects led to 525 separate charges.

The first half of the 17th century was especially prone. In the 1640s, Western Europe was convulsed by war, rebellion, and economic crisis – the setting for active witch-hunts in France, especially Champagne, Languedoc, Ardennes, Gascony, and Burgundy. This caused disquiet. In July 1644, the archbishop of Reims related how innocent people were:

> maltreated, driven out, or physically attacked; they are burned, while it has become customary to take the suspects and throw them into water, then if they float it is enough to make them witches. This is such a great abuse that up to thirty or forty are found in a single parish.

The years 1643–4 and 1649–50 produced intense panics in Scotland, notably East Lothian, where 200 people were burned in 1649 alone. In England, suspected witches were rounded up in Newcastle-upon-Tyne, 1649–50, but this was a modest affair compared to the 300 accusations in the eastern counties in 1645–7, of which more in a moment. As we saw in the last chapter, some countries (such as Poland and Hungary) had their witch-panics very late, even into the 18th century.

An outbreak in Sweden – one of the great, late, witch-panics – is revealing. This occurred in the district of Dalarna, 1668–71, and for a long time was misunderstood because an account written by the vicar of Mora, the village at the eye of the storm, was published inaccurately in several editions. This is what really happened. Confessions in the parish of Älvdalen spread to Mora, and a special commission was set up. Officials interrogated 60 suspects, 21 of whom were beheaded and burned. If this brought catharsis to Dalarna, it was short-lived. Successful witch-trials confirmed to potential accusers the presence of witches, encouraging them to act. Rather than allaying local fears, witch-hunts spread them. Public clamour in the wake of the executions led to another commission in 1671, the cause of more executions. From here, suspicions travelled through the rest of Sweden for another five years.

The abundance of confessions suggests coercion, probably irregular coercion. Abuse of torture, local government, and excessive witch-hunting were closely related. The geometric progression of confessions and accusations was often driven by fear and pain. It also helped if law officers were pro-active, like Mora commissioner Lorentz Creutz. A localized witch-scare in Somerset between 1657 and 1664, overseen by a zealous magistrate named Robert Hunt, produced spectacular confessions. Hunt may have used force, but of course that wasn't recorded. In 1609, hearing that witchcraft plagued the Basque country south of Bordeaux, Henry IV of France sent two judges to investigate. One, Pierre de Lancre, was obsessed with Bodin's idea that a demonic sect was undermining the Christian state, a fear borne out by the hundreds of testimonies and confessions he was required to consider. Elsewhere, witchfinders, at best semi-official in status, helped stir things up. Some, like those working in East Lothian, Newcastle, and northern France, pricked suspects' flesh looking for insensible marks.

Witch-scares devastated communities, but seen in context they are the exceptions that prove the rule, the rule being that they were rare. Nor can we always assume some singular motivating force or personality – a Creutz, a Hunt, or a de Lancre. The Scottish trials of 1661–2 formed a loose pattern of 600 accusations without central impetus; the same was true in Sweden. In the age of state-building, a concerted witch-hunt was an aberration, an abnormal response to abnormal conditions and likely to exacerbate social division to the detriment of order. Pressures from below could be considerable; but this was why governors had to resist them. Rage behind the Alpine trials of 1428 followed the devastation of crops, as in the Bavarian district of Schongau in 1589 when peasant delegations demanded witch-burnings from their masters. The East Anglian panic of the 1640s released pent-up anger about witches from the previous decade, a time of religious conflict, economic gloom, and judicial indifference. But surrender to plebeian passions ran counter to what rulers were trying to achieve: the imposition of government upon community, law upon custom, *Gesellschaft* upon *Gemeinschaft*.

The feminist historian Anne Llewellyn Barstow blamed the 'witch-craze' on the displacement of community courts by state courts. This is misleading. Although state law allowed for witch-hunts, few states promoted them, and even then rarely in a sustained or uncontested way. It is also true that, as historians of southern Germany have argued, some witch-hunts – the principality of Eichstätt is a case in point – were entirely top-down impositions, obviating the need for bottom-up sociological explanations. And yet typically these were small jurisdictions unrepresentative of majority opinion across the Holy Roman Empire. Jenny Gibbons, a modern pagan, has criticized Barstow thus:

> although it has become commonplace to think of the outbreaks of witch hunting as malevolent pogroms imposed by evil elites, in reality the worst horrors occurred where central authority had broken down.

Likewise, witch-hunts ended when central authorities stepped in. After years of incompetent commissions achieving nothing except

11. Witchfinder Matthew Hopkins interrogates Essex suspects in 1645. The peculiar creatures are diabolical familiars

chaos, the Dalarna scare was finally spiked by a court in Stockholm. In Bordeaux, Pierre de Lancre's evidence was undermined by the *Parlement*. Robert Hunt's war against witches in Somerset culminated not in an explosive trial, but the intervention of officials to prevent one. This was in 1665, with the

East Anglian outrages within living memory. Matthew Hopkins, and his partner John Stearne, had exploited wartime disruption of the assizes to style themselves instruments of justice. This led to about 100 executions – one-fifth of England's total for the early modern period – but even then evidence was received sceptically, and the witchfinders' antics not tolerated for long. Initially, the confessions they extracted were compelling; but their methods and pretence to authority were rebarbative. The Scottish witch-hunt of the early 1660s was terminated when the Privy Council limited commissions of judiciary, and cracked down on torture and witchfinders.

Late witch-panics demonstrate something surprising: the high-point of a nation's trials and their decline arrived together. For sure, acting upon belief in the witch-peril encouraged accusations, but it also exposed the difficulty of proving them in a fair and orderly way. The two could not be reconciled, and in the end doubt displaced enthusiasm. This can be seen in the German town of Langenburg, where the execution of Anna Schmieg in 1672 was possible only after an arduous process of investigation, academic debate, and special pleading by the authorities, resulting in permission to torture Schmieg until she confessed. The political context was always significant. In Langenburg, this consisted of the nexus of relationships between peasants, their landlord (and governor), the law court, the universities of Altdorf and Strasbourg, and the Holy Roman Emperor himself. The Würzburg trials cannot be understood outside the machinations of power in the diocese.

Some witch-hunts resulted directly from political problems; whether they were conscious manipulations of law and belief is usually unclear. Some of the worst panics in southern Germany followed the aggressive restoration of Catholicism by Counter-Reformation dukes and prince-bishops. Courts in Jutland (Denmark) promoted witch-trials to deflect criticism about high grain prices. Matthew Hopkins's campaign was not connected to the skulduggery of a royalist spy-network as suggested in 'the

Tendring witchcraft revelations', a document invented in the 1970s by Richard Deacon; and yet as a puritan campaign in a war that was spiritual as well as military, it was necessarily political in character. In Scotland, the North Berwick trials of the 1590s concerned treason cloaked as witchcraft; but this isn't to say that royal consternation was insincere. Demonology and state ideology merged: James the absolutist monarch and James the witch-hunter were the same man on the same royal business. Cases of mass demonic possession also sprang from power struggles. The hysterical behaviour of nuns at Loudun in the 1630s, and the execution of the priest Urbain Grandier, had roots in factional strife, as did shocking outbursts at the convent of Santa Chiara in Carpi, northern Italy, in 1636.

In the developing world today, witch-hunts further political ends, usually without much hope that central authority will stop things getting out of hand. Too often, the lawlessness that feeds campaigns of terror is endemic. In the 20th century, colonial powers like the British in Africa and Dutch in Indonesia tried to stamp out witch-hunting, an imposition of the rule of law detested as a white man's amnesty for witches. Witch-hunts were therefore acts of resistance and, in the post-colonial era, demonstrations of independence. The 'revitalization movements' and 'purification cults' studied by anthropologists, programmes of spiritual and cultural renewal involving witch-hunting, predate European presence but became bound up with the politics of imperialism and decolonization. India, South-East Asia, Central and South America, and the Indian reservations of the USA have all known witch-hunting in the modern era.

Civil war in Africa produces festering panics. In recent times, witch-hunting has blighted, among other places, Ghana, Malawi, Zaire, Kenya, Congo, Zambia, Nigeria, Tanzania, Uganda, and South Africa's northern province. In Zimbabwe, Robert Mugabe's ZANU soldiers allied themselves to witchfinders to win support and intimidate opponents. After Angola declared independence in

1975, the Marxist MPLA party tried to suppress the persecutions common during more than a decade of guerrilla fighting. They failed, and US-backed rebels continued to help locals hunt witches into the 21st century; families were required to look happy as they watched relatives being executed. Such ghastly stories remind us not only of the proximity and relevance of witch-panics in the world today, but of the suffering experienced by the accused, past as well as present. It mattered not a bit to Anna Schmieg that she was the last witch to be executed in Langenburg, nor would the Essex and Suffolk folk condemned by Hopkins have cared that his reign of terror would last less than two years.

This section ends as it began: with a letter, also from Germany in the 1620s, but this time from a father to his daughter. The father was Johannes Junius, mayor of Bamberg until he was sucked into his city's witch-panic and, in breach of imperial rules, forced to confess his diabolism. With hands broken by thumbscrews, Junius scrawled an account of his torments, protesting his innocence and lamenting that 'whosoever comes into the witch prison must become a witch or be tortured until he invents something out of his head'. Veronica Junius never saw her father's letter. It was intercepted and added to his file, part of the body of evidence that led to him being burned shortly afterwards.

Children

The grief of persecution cannot be quantified. What emotional and material damage was caused to the Junius family and thousands like them? They, too, were victims of the witch-hunt. Yet to understand witch-hunting, remember from an emic rather than an etic perspective the victims were those who suffered at the hands of witches. It's true that during panics, when all sorts of people were accused, men like the chancellor at Würzburg perceived a massacre of the innocents not a righteous war against Satan. These were exceptional events, however, and in the normal run of witch-trials far more rage was directed at witches than at their persecutors. If we accept the contemporary reality of a divine–diabolic cosmology, as we should, then this violent hatred is comprehensible, especially whenever the witch's victim was a child.

Some believe that, in an age of high infant mortality, parents rarely formed strong emotional bonds with their children. This is false. Richard Napier, a 17th-century English physician and astrologer, treated many women suffering from 'disturbing grief' caused by losing children. In Chapter 3, we saw how the Durrant family of Essex was torn apart by the death of a two-year-old boy attributed to *maleficium*. In 1646, in the Norfolk parish of Upwell, the children of Robert and Katherine Parsons, aged seven years and twenty-four weeks respectively, died within three weeks of each other. Katherine Parsons's grief turned to fury, triggering the accusation of Ellen Garrison, a woman long suspected of witchcraft. The Durrant and Parsons cases were part of the wider witch-panic directed by the witchfinders Hopkins and Stearne.

Many young mothers experience feelings of insecurity, which historically have been projected onto witches. The Greeks and Romans believed that children were vulnerable to the evil eye – the witch's gaze – and protective amulets are still used today. Plutarch explained that children were not yet strong enough to resist malefic magic. In the early modern period, nuggets of coral were used as counter-magical teethers, and in 18th-century Amsterdam you could buy a printed charm to protect a mother and newborn baby. This anxiety was displayed more actively. Around 1609, Susan Barber of New Romney in Kent was resting after giving birth when, she claimed, diabolical imps belonging to her sinister landlord (William Godfrey: see Chapter 4) tried to drag her baby away; hearing screams, Barber's husband rushed in to find her clutching its ankles. The child sex-abuse scandals of the 1980s can be seen in a similar light: parental love manifested as fear.

The evil eye has long been associated with jealousy over children. The liminality of certain female life-stages – the unmarried adolescent, the mother during childbirth, the menopausal wife or widow – might in people's minds place women in the company of witches, who could be either their friends or enemies. Historians have identified inter-generational conflict in witchcraft accusations, even within households. Writing about 17th-century Augsburg, Lyndal Roper has shown how 'lying-in maids' attending a birth were sometimes seen as envious inversions of the ideal mother. Walpurga Hausmännin, a midwife in the German town of Dillingen, was executed in 1587 for having sex with Satan and murdering forty-four children. However, the idea that midwives were commonly accused, popularized in a book by Barbara Ehrenreich and Deirdre English, has been exaggerated. In England, at least, most midwives featuring in witchcraft investigations were experts on the teats suckled by imps, and so appeared as witnesses rather than defendants.

Children who survived witch-attacks gave evidence against their tormentors. In Yorkshire, in 1661, James Johnson, an eleven-year-old servant, was the star witness against a witch, who, he said, had caused him to excrete stones ranging in size from a cherry pip to a pigeon's egg. Johnson may have been manipulated; doubtless his master knew that children seemed like innocent conduits of truth. But their fertile imaginations were also a source of injustice. The Dalarna panic began with tales of the sabbat told by Gertrud Svensdotter, aged eleven like James Johnson. Adults, conscious of the Devil's guile and frantic to discover witches, took children unusually seriously – something that must have appealed to children. Minors even became witchfinders. In the Burgundy witch-hunt of 1644–5, a shepherd boy dubbed 'the little prophet' identified witches, and in the Lancashire scare of 1634, Edmund Robinson was taken by his father from church to church where he stood on a stall looking for suspects. Ten-year-old Robinson swore to magistrates he had been abducted to a sabbat, and named at least fifteen witches. Interrogated in London, however, the boy confessed to fraud and his father was imprisoned.

The social psychologist Hans Sebald wrote a book about children's suggestibility as legal witnesses, rooting his analysis in early modern witch-hunts. Among credulous adults, the 'mythomanical child', unable to tell fantasy from reality, can unconsciously devastate innocent lives. This has been seen in modern child-abuse cases, and in early modern demonic possessions. Claims made by the Throckmorton children in the Huntingdonshire village of Warboys led to the execution of Alice and John Samuel and their daughter Agnes in 1593. The girls, the eldest of whom was fifteen, suffered illness attributed to evil spirits infiltrating their bodies. Such symptoms could be learned: a pamphlet about the Throckmorton case was read in at least two other households where children were 'possessed' in the early 17th century. These stories suggest the peculiar anxiety that witchcraft stirred in parents, but also the difficulties faced by children in hierarchical societies and repressive families. They had to make the transition to independence by asserting themselves without breaking social rules. Mixed with brewing suspicions about witchcraft, the combination could be explosive.

Typical of the ambiguity of witchcraft, some children were saintly victims, some malicious dreamers, and others witches. Abandonment of the stereotype during panics was a particular cause of such accusations; children accounted for 70% of the 1,800 Basque suspects in 1609–11. Many were scolded; others were less fortunate. In the city of Trier, a boy named Matthias was tortured into confessing that he had attended a sabbat where the vice-governor, Dr Dietrich Flade, was present; Flade was burned – the most senior official to die in the European witch-hunt. Children were executed too. The chancellor of Würzburg wrote: 'I have seen put to death children of seven, promising students of ten, twelve, fourteen and fifteen'; some as young as three were accused. A quarter of the 160 witches executed in Würzburg, 1627–9, were juveniles. Some children were tarred by the parental brush, like the nine-year-old Suffolk boy who confessed to covenanting with Satan after his mother was hanged as a witch, or the two children executed in Saxony after their father's conviction. Witchcraft was thought to be an inheritable condition, and children grew up dreading the day of accusation. This belief remains current. Evans-Pritchard noticed how the sons of male Azande witches were all witches, likewise the daughters of female witches.

In Nigeria, thousands of children have been persecuted by evangelical preachers and prophets, and either killed or exiled. Today, many live under the protection of the Child Rights and Rehabilitation Network, a separate community – like the so-called 'witch-villages' of Ghana – run by a British charity. These beliefs, a blend of Christianity and African folklore, travel with migrants to the developed world. In the UK, there are several hundred fundamentalist churches of west African origin where supposedly possessed people are exorcised. Children are frequently seen as *kendoki* – witches – and abused accordingly. Almost sixty cases were reported to the Metropolitan Police between 2006 and 2008. In London in 2000, eight-year-old Victoria Climbié was tortured to death by her guardians after she was denounced as a witch by a local pastor.

Salem's lot

Hans Sebald refers to 'Salem syndrome': the child's propensity to believe fantasies about the criminal guilt of adults, leading to miscarriages of justice. But at the Salem trials – in Massachusetts in 1692, the most famous witch-panic – the 'victims' were not adults but the children bewitched by adults. Some had died. Samuel Gray testified that an apparition of a witch appeared in his house one night, causing his baby to scream; from that time his 'very lively, thriving child did pine away'. Directing the ensuing drama, as in Arthur Miller's *The Crucible* (1953), were the girls who writhed in the courtroom, tortured by demons sent by the defendants. Although Miller was none too concerned with historical accuracy, by studying the court records he infused his play with the atmospheric pressure and terrifying, inescapable logic of a witch-hunt.

Another important character in *The Crucible* is Tituba, a West Indian household slave, whose confession lights the fuse. As in the real story, she represents the 'other': an alien culture of superstition and malevolence. From the time of the first permanent settlements in America, the English had interpreted native religion as satanic paganism, a mark of inferiority which helped justify massacres and land appropriations. In *Good Newes from Virginia* (1613), godly migrant Alexander Whitaker derided Indian shamans as 'no other but such as our English witches are'. By 'witches', he probably meant cunning folk, but other observers detected a more explicitly diabolic streak. Taken prisoner by Nipmuck warriors in the 1670s, Mary Rowlandson witnessed a war-dance in which the *powwaw*, or shaman, looked 'as black as the Devil' and was no less infernal in his rituals. As Rowlandson discovered during her captivity, European colonists redefined themselves in the wilderness, and the 'other' – different, disturbing, demonic – was held up as a mirror of a divided self, caught between the old world and the new.

Before 1692, there had been few witchcraft prosecutions in America. Previously, the largest trials were in 1651 in Bermuda, and in 1662, at Hartford, Connecticut. At Hartford, eleven people were formally accused; at Salem more than 150. New England saw hardly any cases in the 1640s, but considerably more in the subsequent decade, although executions were rare: just four of the Hartford witches were hanged. In the following quarter of a century, there were three convictions (from over forty prosecutions), and all of those were subsequently reversed. Confessions were virtually unheard of.

What happened at Salem, then, was extraordinary. The crisis began in February 1692 in the household of Samuel Parris, a minister in the small agricultural community of Salem Village. His daughter and niece were the initial victims, and Tituba was his slave. Accusations spread swiftly through Essex County. Half the accused lived in Salem or nearby Andover, but twenty-four townships were involved. By May, when the new governor of Massachusetts, William Phips, appointed a special court to investigate, some fifty suspects were in custody. Many confessed to confederacy with the Devil, perhaps because only people refusing to confess were executed; those who, in effect, perjured themselves were spared. By the time the trials were stopped in October, nineteen had been hanged and one crushed to death for refusing to plead. In *The Crucible*, John Proctor dies because he tears up his confession, saying: 'How may I live without my name?'

Many have tried to explain Salem: historians, novelists, playwrights, and scientists; there are dozens of books on the subject. Here are a few of the headings under which John Demos, a historian of early America, summarizes interpretations: divine retribution (a contemporary rationale); period piece (Salem as

12. George Jacobs is accused of witchcraft by his own granddaughter at Salem. He was executed 19 August 1692

'strange kind of romantic myth'); deception (i.e. fraud by the alleged victims); class conflict; village factionalism; cultural provincialism (and anti-puritanism); the coming of capitalism; political repression; mental illness; epidemic illness; vulnerability of children; 'acid trip'. Some theories are more plausible than others. 'Acid trip' – the idea that victims ate rye infected with ergot, a psychotropic fungus – has captured the public imagination. But the problem, as with mental illness and deception, is that this doesn't so much explain Salem as explain it *away*. Here we return to two earlier points: witchcraft accusations as hysteria, and as a scam to grab property – both popular theories about Salem. Again, we are told what witchcraft was *really* about to save us from having to accept the power of contemporary belief. In the end, Salem may *really* have been about witchcraft.

Once more, the emic jostles with the etic. Today some of the most sophisticated research concerns the relationship between politics and emotion in an era of change. Salem has long been understood in terms of warring factions, the struggling conservatives of Salem Village set against the more prosperous and worldly Salem Town – God versus Mammon, Puritan versus Yankee. The witch-trials were a birthpang of modern America, a painful accommodation between piety and civility, on the one hand, and physical and spiritual wilderness, on the other. It is an attractive idea, though perhaps too neat. Recent work suggests that the economic and geographical divides at Salem were less clear-cut than Paul Boyer and Stephen Nissenbaum proposed in their ground-breaking study *Salem Possessed* (1974); but this remains controversial. Boyer and Nissenbaum's reliance on a tax list of 1695 to assess the opponents' relative wealth may be misleading.

Without doubt, Salem was made possible by factors familiar from elsewhere. First, remoteness from central government: Westminster was 3,000 miles away. At this date not every English judge would have admitted 'spectral evidence', and making confession a qualification for forgiveness bizarrely reversed

European convention. Second, political insecurity. Massachusetts had been rudderless since the governor was overthrown during the English revolution of 1688–9, and losing its colonial charter in 1684 had undermined the legitimacy of justice. Third, involvement of clergymen in local affairs. Like most crazes, Salem was not about the growth of the state but its weakness and failure.

Yet this only makes sense if we restore anxiety, rage, and belief to the equation. In a sermon of 1689, Cotton Mather articulated Old World fears dating back to Bodin that 'the vultures of hell' were preying on Christian society. Mather knew of the Dalarna witch-hunt, and understood that the Devil would fight most viciously godly intruders in his own land: America. What Mather called the 'hideous wretches in hideous horrors confessing' were incontrovertible proof. In fact, a real war was in progress, one inevitably seen in providential–diabolical terms. The Anglo-Indian conflict of the mid-1670s had delivered a devastating psychic shock, leaving colonists trembling, waiting for the next attack. The worlds of demons and native warriors merged, especially in the minds of children. In her book of 2002, Mary Beth Norton proved the significance of this fear, compounded by the outbreak in 1689 of hostilities on Massachusetts' northern border. Many of the principal figures in the Salem panic had personal experience of these traumas, helping to cement the physical and spiritual worlds of danger essential to all witch-trials.

For a few months in 1692, witchcraft became terrifyingly real at Salem. George Burroughs, an accused minister, defended himself using arguments from Thomas Ady's *Candle in the Dark*, a sceptical book published after the English trials in the 1640s. But to no avail: the fear of witches was greater than fear of injustice, and he was hanged. Then, suddenly, proceedings were stopped by political fiat and the soul-searching began. Governor Phips had been advised by Increase Mather, Cotton's more judicious father, who believed 'it were better that ten suspected witches should escape, than that one innocent person should be condemned'.

Within a few years, a pardon was granted, the jurors recanted, and a judge apologized. Samuel Parris, in whose household the crisis had begun, was forced to resign. Far from alleviating New England's problems, wrote one critic, Salem had poured oil on the flames.

Salem is another example of how some of the worst witch-panics happened just as the reality of witchcraft as a crime was abating. In particular, it shows how finely balanced was the argument separating the necessity of finding proof to fight Satan and the ultimate impossibility of that. Here we return to an earlier point about witchcraft and modernity. The witnesses at Salem may have been hysterical, but the bench – sober men of erudition and reason – was not. Hard though it is to accept now, Mather, Hathorne, and the rest were pushing boundaries to do right in what they saw as the most difficult and urgent crisis to affect their colony, mankind even. 'The events of Salem mark the eruption of not an atavistic spiritual irrationality', argues Sarah Rivett, 'but rather the reverse: the application of a rationality that presented new empirical potential'. The judges were wrong and before long they knew it, but the new mood of intellectual endeavour would endure. Endorsing spectral evidence and banishing it were part of the same transition, and for decades co-existed. By 1750, however, the line between the spiritual and the material, fantasy and reality, had shifted decisively towards that commonly shared by most adults in the Western world today.

Chapter 7
Fantasy

The reality problem

You might imagine that the backlash killed off Salem's belief in witches. But it was not the reality of witchcraft that was under attack, so much as the status of its evidence. On the surface, the letter written by the chancellor of Würzburg in 1629 looks sceptical, ahead of its time; but we shouldn't miss the author's postscript stating 'beyond doubt' that elsewhere in Germany the Devil had officiated at a black mass for 8,000, using turnip peelings instead of the Holy Eucharist. At Langenburg, where Anna Schmieg was executed in 1672, the reality of witchcraft was poised between its tangible presence and absolute non-existence as a crime that could be proved without risk of injustice – Increase Mather's concern at Salem. To get its conviction, the Langenburg court had to declare witchcraft *crimen exceptum* in all but name, forcing the distinction in order to make witchcraft both substantial and attributable to an individual.

Historians, too, have to face the reality problem: how to take seriously that which they reject ontologically. Witchcraft has been called the historical subject with a hole in the middle. As we've seen, from the 1970s historians returned to the primary sources, restoring all forms of magic as ideas that once had made sense. Contrary to rationalist condescension, belief deserved explanation. Then, in the

1990s, it became clear that saying what was really happening in witchcraft narratives was not the same as saying what early modern people *thought* was happening. A lot of very competent research now seemed like a comfortable rationalization suited to a modern audience. Who are *we*, asked some, to tell *them* what was going on? David Harley, a historian who exploded the myth of the midwife-witch, pointed to 'an epistemological problem at the heart of most histories of witchcraft that makes it difficult for historians to hear the explanations offered at the time'. Historians today are certainly better at this than they were half a century ago, but the fact remains that demonology is deceptively hard to read without sensitivity to cultural context and a powerful leap of imagination.

But then demonology was hard to read in its own time, and by 1700 differences of interpretation separated the educated elite from the common people, and sections of the elite from each another. We saw something of the latter in the Glanvill–Webster and Bodin–Weyer controversies. These positions were not sharply defined. In the 1660s, the believer Joseph Glanvill admitted that 'the great body of mankind is very credulous, and in this matter so that they do believe vain impossible things'. Yet critics, even those who believed in the Devil, felt his opinions were no less vain and impossible – a sign of the boundless relativity of witch-beliefs. A surprising number of trials took place in England in these decades. Witchcraft remained plausible but with hardly any convictions, suggesting a failure of confidence in proof. And just as executions had once advertised the existence of witches, so an absence of executions diminished their reality.

Possession cases were drained of demonic significance. In Chapter 4, we saw how early Stuart monarchs played down the exorcistic claims of Catholics and puritans alike, inhibiting *the* great set-piece drama of diabolism. An alleged possession would have been the closest most people came to direct experience of malevolent supernature. By the 1680s, there were even fewer demons clamouring for attention. English Tories, proponents of divine right monarchy and the Anglican Church, defended the truth of such episodes more than their Whig opponents whose views were reformist, parliamentary, low church. (That said, dissenting ministers extolled the charismatic virtue of exorcism well into the 18th century.) The Whig–Tory divide also shaped the debate over witchcraft. Tory reactionaries were increasingly out of step, culturally and intellectually, with early Enlightenment thinking. From Whigs and the fashion-conscious came mockery of the credulous lower orders and the learned men who shared their beliefs. After the Salem trials, a local merchant named Thomas Brattle, later a fellow of the Royal Society, told a friend that his townsmen were the laughing stock of 'the reasonable part of the world'.

Having dispensed with witchcraft as an actionable crime, the reasonable part of the world turned on its theoretical reality. Hobbes had called demons metaphors for evil; Spinoza denied the very existence of evil. The cry of atheism against such men lost its sting. The dualism of René Descartes (the separation of body and soul or mind), and a 'mechanical' philosophy of the universe (whereby natural phenomena obey laws of nature) were widely accepted; God seemed less of a providential tyrant, more a benign architect guided by reason. In the 1690s, a Dutch Cartesian named Balthasar Bekker published *De Betoverde Weereld*, translated as *The World Bewitched*. God's love was supreme, reasoned Bekker, and the Devil was a miserable, impotent figure – exactly the opposite argument to that of his sceptical predecessor Johann Weyer. In *De Crimine Magiae* (1701), Christian Thomasius, a German law professor, maintained that witchcraft was a clerical invention. Then in 1718, Bishop Francis Hutchinson attributed witches to 'the imaginations of men'; witch-ordeals, he said, were 'the meanest of paganish and popish superstitions', spectral evidence 'far from being legal proof'.

Once philosophical scepticism had become a hallmark of enlightened thought, legislators were bound to fall into step, often long after their judges. France repealed its witchcraft statute in 1682; Prussia, 1714; England and Scotland, 1736; Russia, 1770; Sweden, 1779. By the later 18th century, witchcraft was self-evidently nonsensical and not worth refuting. Voltaire considered occult phenomena irrelevant to the operation of nature, and a symbol of medieval superstition. Meanwhile, witch-beliefs remained part of plebeian culture in Europe, and linger in pockets to this day. I once lived in a village near Cambridge where *maleficium*, charms, violent counter-magic, and diabolic imps were current in the 1920s. Writers who condemned such survivals as barbaric madness symbolized the 'division of cultures' that occurred in the 18th and 19th centuries. And not just that, but a division of perceived *realities* – much as colonial African societies were distanced from their imperial overlords.

Most Western people have inherited a basic Enlightenment epistemology, which is why writing about witches is so tricky. Anthropology reminds us that not everyone made the same intellectual journey. Traditional witch-beliefs are resistant to innovations in thinking because their basis is emotional and material, their rationale instinctive. Evans-Pritchard struggled to discuss witchcraft with the Azande because their beliefs and ideas were 'imprisoned in action'. Such relativism teaches us that *subjectivity* of witchcraft is at least as important as the outsider's *objective* view. This has been called 'the experiential dimension'. Here the reality of witchcraft is no problem to the people who live unquestioningly in that reality, and should not be made into one.

Experiencing witchcraft

Here's some more early modern reality. Remember Robert and Katherine Parsons of Upwell, who attributed their children's deaths to Ellen Garrison's witchcraft? Guided by Matthew Hopkins, Garrison was detained by her neighbours and was watched carefully. Avis Savory, a shoemaker's wife, was one of several witnesses who saw 'a thing in likeness of a beetle come into the room'. This she judged to be a demonic familiar, as did fellow watchers, one of whom killed it. Its place was taken by a cricket that, Savory believed, had crawled down the chimney. She also saw suspicious teats on Garrison's body, and accepted the witchfinder's opinion 'that some of the Devil's imps had sucked her'.

There is no reason to suppose that Avis Savory and her neighbours were lying, and to call them deluded only makes an anachronistic comparison with ourselves. We might return to Marina Warner's point that the supernatural exists 'without ascertainable outside referents'; and where historical stories of the occult are concerned, this means us as well as the solid things of past society. There is no reason why our mentalities should be used as a framework for interpreting what Upwell thought in 1646. What matters is the parish's experience and what this meant – their subjectivity. We tend to be more concerned with factual 'truth' (etic) than with relevance to culture (emic) because it is easier to grasp the former than it is to demonstrate the latter. Ellen Garrison's story is part of the wider story of her community; the question is: how did they fit together? Possession cases need the same careful treatment. The historian of the Santa Chiara episode warns against anachronism and reductionism: cutting a 17th-century story from 21st-century cloth. The nuns' own perceptions of their 'troubling experiences' are significant. Sarah Ferber, an expert on exorcism in early modern France, has argued that the historical reality of possession was just what the documents describe.

Reaction against reductionist histories of witchcraft has a precedent. In the 19th century, alongside rationalism grew romanticism and with it the idea that witches had been a real sect, benign, passionate, and persecuted – the women Margaret Murray raised to mythological significance in the 1920s. In Europe's age of revolutions, anti-clericalism, and secular statehood, the church was blamed for all sorts of cruel injustices including witch-hunting. This had been the main beef of the German lawyer Thomasius. Now Jacob Grimm, collector of the famous fairy tales, portrayed

13. A romantic vision of Circe, sorceress from Greek mythology, by
Pre-Raphaelite artist J. W. Waterhouse

witches as wise women, an idea elaborated by the French historian Jules Michelet (1798–1874), who repackaged them as proto-revolutionary heroines battling feudal oppression. Historical novels, notably those by Sir Walter Scott, mixed fact with fiction. William Harrison Ainsworth's *The Lancashire Witches* (1849) turned a well-documented 17th-century witch-hunt into a gothic romance. Fantasy and reality converged in the public imagination, just as they had while the witch-trials were still in progress.

The destruction of Margaret Murray owed much to two historians: Norman Cohn, who had exposed Lamothe-Langon's bogus witch-hunt; and Hugh Trevor-Roper, later embroiled in a hoax of his own, the Hitler diaries. Cohn and Trevor-Roper stood between rationalism and relativism, in other words condemning witch-hunting as an idea but ready to understand it intellectually as a form of past reality. Both men had witnessed persecution first hand in the Second World War and were fiercely opposed to totalitarianism. Plus the Nazis had endorsed pagan ideals to highlight the church's oppression of authentic *völkish* culture. Like all folklore, the idea that witch-beliefs were noble traditions became unfashionable – even suspect – to the postwar generation. We saw earlier that some historians like Carlo Ginzburg looked for traces of the social and religious reality of witchcraft in the archives. But as Ginzburg was writing, around 1990, another historiographical development arrived: the linguistic or cultural 'turn', promoting close analysis of texts to uncover concealed meanings. Rationalist grand narratives of history fragmented into a kaleidoscope of perspectives and interpretations, united only as 'discourse'. Ambiguity and possibility replaced authority and certainty. Now one postmodern version of reality competed, or at least co-existed, with another.

Postmodernism encouraged a psychoanalytic approach to witchcraft present in the works of Sigmund Freud and Carl Jung. Jung understood the focii of spiritual beliefs as signs of a collective unconscious, a common pool of images he called 'archetypes'.

Freud's theories concentrated on the psychopathology of the individual. In the case of the possessed 17th-century artist Johann Christoph Haizmann, Freud diagnosed a castration complex resulting from his father's death; as we've seen, Freud also hailed Johann Weyer as a pioneer of psychiatry. This was all rather anachronistic, imposing a modern reality on an early modern one. But postmodernism encouraged a more sensitive historical analysis of witchcraft, one that took seriously the subjectivity not just of accusers but of suspects. Both belonged to the same mental world, and many witches were accusers themselves. Lyndal Roper saw in the confessions of witches in Augsburg evidence not just of learned demonology instilled by torture, but the emotions and ambitions of ordinary women. Confessions are stories, and stories are the key to unlocking the mysteries of inner lives in the past as in the present.

Witchcraft was occult power, there for the taking and, from shame and a desire for redemption, weak and desperate people who had helped themselves confessed. This might explain why not all confessing suspects were tortured or deranged. Witches at Salem admitted their crimes without torture, nor were they just sacrificing their names to save their skins. At least one explained that she had allied herself to the Devil in return for his protection from Indian attack. In his investigations, Bordeaux judge Pierre de Lancre probably didn't torture either; he merely listened to the countless tales of what has been called the 'Basque dream epidemic'. Étienne Delcambre, an archivist who combed the Lorraine records in the 1950s, noticed how idiosyncratic confessions were: some confessed without torture or after withstanding it; others admitted serious charges while strenuously denying the petty stuff. Robin Briggs, who followed up Delcambre's work, sees feelings encoded as fantasies, 'a form of imaginative revenge ... an expression of psychic realism on the part of their makers'; he also detects signs of narcissism, infantilism, and masochism. Focusing especially on the psycho-social causation of disease, Edward Bever makes an extreme case for the lived reality of witchcraft – a reality independent from the descriptive language of demonologists, judges, and historians.

All this goes too far for some. David Hall doubts that events in 1692 were rooted in the psychic disturbance of puritan New England, as has been suggested, predicting that most people would prefer an explanation based on 'a commonsense psychology of guilt and projection'. Modern theorization can distort historical contexts. Critics of Lyndal Roper dispute that confessions were 'collective fantasies' constructed from the dialogue between prisoners and inquisitors, however much the former wanted to establish the authenticity of their stories. One historian objects to using the terms 'fantasy' and 'reality', because the modern distinction between them cannot be projected backwards. Again, we hit against Wittgenstein's 'bewitchment of our intelligence by means of language': we are either misled by words or hamstrung by them. On the other hand, the 'experiential dimension' is too zealously observed when *any* historical intervention is seen to contaminate the historical reality of the supernatural.

We don't have to embrace psychoanalysis as an historical tool to appreciate the autobiographical qualities of confessions. Women and men told compelling stories of their lives, full of desire and disappointment, anger and frustration. In 1645, Essex teenager Rebecca West didn't just have sex with the Devil: reader, she married him. Tituba, Samuel Parris's slave, described Satan as a forceful suitor offering a yellow bird and other 'pretty things'. Who knows, perhaps she'd never received a gift before. Pierre de Lancre was horrified by witches' sensual pleasure. 'Instead of keeping quiet about this damnable coupling', he fumed, 'they recount the dirtiest and most obscene occurrences with such liberty and gaiety that they make saying it glorious'. Demonology, then, might be a holiday from misery. Revenge and sex aside, fantasies centred on food. At the sabbat attended by the maidservant Anne Armstrong, cheese, beef, mutton, and capon were served, as well as 'the plum broth the capon was boiled in'. Hungry, downtrodden people make extravagant fantasists.

Magic redux

By 1700, forced confessions were frequently dismissed at law, and voluntary ones taken to signify mental illness. The rationalism that saved suspects from the gallows was worth having, however condescendingly voiced in public. 'Woman, you do confess impossible things, as that you turn yourselves into cats', a lady told a Kentish witch in 1692, 'it cannot be'. She and two wretched companions were tried but acquitted.

Scepticism has been as a badge of reason ever since. Between the 18th and 20th centuries, it served historians and social scientists well, even if today it can seem patronizing. Evans-Pritchard and Trevor-Roper leavened their rationalism with relativism, but basically saw witch-beliefs as a primitivism from which their society had escaped. The sociologist Max Weber (1864–1920) wrote of a 'disenchantment of the world', whereby witchcraft was swept away by a wave of secularization. European states grew more confident, better governed, protected by police and armies; they felt less threatened by apocalyptic forces. Churches were made to accept religious toleration, and the universe seemed more ordered. Power was invested in worldly things like capitalism, industry, science, and technology; economic growth undermined the peasant's 'limited good'. Yet Weber's thesis only works if the world disenchanted means the prosperous, educated world of the Western urban elite. Even then, the picture is not always sharply drawn.

Who believed in witchcraft in 1900? By different definitions, almost the entire human race. Just as Matthew Hopkins's ideas lived on in my old village in the 1920s, the 16th-century world of Ginzburg's *benandanti* was still thriving in Italy in the 1940s. Carlo Levi, a doctor exiled to a remote backwater, wrote of peasants who saw goats as satanic, contacted spirits to find treasure, and used spells in everyday life; the priest had given up on 'that closed world, shrouded in black veils, bloody and earthy'. Levi looked at his countrymen with detached curiosity, like Evans-Pritchard among the Azande, or our Kentish gentlewoman in 1692. And, as we saw earlier, in the 1970s the French Bocage region was alive with such 'archaic' ideas and practices. Even today, belief in magic and witches still belongs to the daily experiences, and subjective impressions, of the greater part of the global population.

There is something quintessentially human about the witch-fantasy. After the trials ended, even educated people remained agnostic. 'To the last, the most radical argument against the witch-craze', Trevor-Roper argued, 'was not that witches do not exist, not even that the pact with Satan is impossible, but simply that judges err in their identification'. To mock witchcraft publicly was not necessarily to be unafraid in private. Plebeian fears, meanwhile, were very public. Most still worked on the land and clung to associated supernatural beliefs; decriminalization caused some to take the law into their own hands. In Britain, the redundancy of the Witchcraft Act led to violent incidents. When in 1695 a man at Tarleton in Lancashire decided that Margaret Hollinghurst was to blame for his poor health, he hit her with a stone; she died the next day. Scots too continued to crave justice for witches. In 1705, people at Pittenweem in Fife, unable to try Janet Cornfoot, crushed her to death with the connivance of local gentry. The Privy Council recommended the prosecution of all involved.

Few things illustrate the division of cultures better than a mob-leader executed for killing a witch, reported in a newspaper the mob couldn't read. A new Witchcraft Act (1736) not only proscribed witch-hunting, but forbade pretence to the conjuration of spirits in order to protect the middle classes from fraudulent fortune-tellers. The lower orders were thus doubly distanced from their social superiors. In 1751, the crowd that saw a butcher hanged for lynching Ruth Osborne at Tring in Hertfordshire grumbled regret that he should die for ridding the land of a wicked witch.

Osborne, like many others, had been subjected to the water ordeal. The following year, a press report of the witch-crazed mobs that swam old women in Suffolk noted that 'it was strange that people should so soon forget the execution at Tring... or forget that there's an Act of Parliament to abolish witches'.

Modern examples are not confined to the developing world, or even to African immigrant communities in Europe. The folklorist Cecil Williamson recalled that in 1915, when he was six years old and staying with an uncle in Devon, he saw four labourers strip an old woman to search her for the Devil's marks. She was only saved because he and his uncle, the local vicar, intervened. Williamson was not an unimpeachable witness, but his story is plausible: a number of assaults on alleged witches in rural England are recorded into the 1920s. Villagers in Germany torched the house of a suspected witch, injuring her and killing her 'diabolic familiars'; that was in 1976. Between 1993 and 1997, at least six witches were beaten or burned to death in Siberia and northern Russia.

Most of the world, then, has remained enchanted. Nor is this just a matter of survivals or continuities of ancient belief. After 1700, witchcraft and magic returned in new forms for the modern age. The romanticism that attracted Grimm, Michelet, and Murray was an emotional and political reaction against the domination of church and state and the soullessness of industrial life. In the 19th and 20th centuries – the age of revolutions – the people reclaimed a measure of power, and *Gesellschaft* made concessions to the ethos of *Gemeinschaft*: blood, soil, and spirit, however cynically those things came to be deployed in state propaganda. Organized religion, though pluralistic, was not yet in marked decline; but church-going, especially its more austere forms, failed to satisfy the spiritual needs of those who desired spectacle, responsivity, and inclusiveness from their faith.

Occultism filled this gap. Aleister Crowley (1875–1947) rebelled against a strict Christian upbringing to study occult literature, notably Waite's *Book of Black Magic and Pacts*. In 1898, Crowley joined the Hermetic Order of the Golden Dawn and excelled as a ritual magician. In 1904, his wife channelled 'Aiwas', an Egyptian holy man, who handed down the Law of Thelema: 'do what thou wilt shall be the whole of the law' – an extreme libertarianism. Crowley spent his life travelling, writing, and exploring the astral plane with collaborators, including various 'scarlet women' with whom he tried (unsuccessfully) to conceive a 'magical child'. In 1945, he ended up in a boarding house on England's south coast where he met Gerald Gardner, the most important figure in the revival of witchcraft. Like Crowley, Gardner came from a well-to-do family and travelled widely. In the Far East, he had discovered beliefs that appealed more than Christianity, and in the 1930s was initiated into a cult whose members claimed descent from early modern witches. His ancestor, he said, was Grissell Gairdner, burned in Scotland in 1610, although this was later disproved. Gardner's story that in 1940 his witches joined forces with other covens to magically prevent Hitler invading England may have been another fantasy. Yet such activity is conceivable, and, if real, was endorsed by the fact of Nazi defeat.

After the war, Gardner used fiction to write about modern witchcraft on the grounds that attempted conjuration was illegal under the 1736 Witchcraft Act. Intended to protect clients of 'witches' against fraud, this statute posed little threat to ritual magicians; but the idea that they were legally persecuted made good publicity. Even so, in 1951 the statute was repealed, and England's witches came out from the forests. Gardner started his own coven and moved to the Isle of Man, where he bought the Museum of Witchcraft from Cecil Williamson – the man who claimed to have rescued a witch from a Devon mob. In 1953, Gardner initiated a witch named Doreen Valiente; when she objected to Crowley's magic they rewrote the rituals, thus forming the basis of modern witchcraft. Gardner's *Witchcraft Today* (1954) put into practice Margaret Murray's idea of witches as a cult; Murray wrote the introduction. The book sold well, inspired hundreds of others to set up covens, and saw Gardner dubbed 'Britain's Chief Witch'. Newspapers were eager to report stories about the occult, as they had during the witch-trials. In the 1960s, the sheep's heart nailed to the church at Castle Rising (see Chapter 3), and similar creepy incidents, led to demands that the Witchcraft Act be reinstated.

Another group who benefited from the repeal of the Witchcraft Act were the Spiritualists. Spiritualism had origins in the theology of Emanuel Swedenbourg, an 18th-century mystic who communed with spirits and demons. Jung's theory of archetypes was partly inspired by his writings. One might see even older antecedents, such as the angelic conversations of Dr John Dee. The modern Spiritualist movement began in mid-19th-century America, drawing on social energies as diverse as evangelicalism, political resistance, popular literacy, and the culture of mourning. Spiritualism travelled to Western Europe, and séances where mediums contacted the dead flourished. Whereas Gerald Gardner would react against the stultifying effect of science on spirituality, Spiritualism embraced it. At a time when Christianity was being challenged (for example by Darwinism), Spiritualism offered freedom from faith, and in its place scientific proof of survival after death. This appealed to middle-class intelligentsia and non-conformist artisans alike: Spiritualism brought together the salon, the laboratory, and the chapel.

Between 1850 and 1950, Spiritualism was so successful that clergymen, dismayed by dwindling congregations, joined in. Perhaps, after all, this was God's truth about salvation, a revelation of eternal life. Not everyone agreed. Many Christians, especially Catholics, condemned Spiritualism as a demonic abomination. The Catholic bishop of Nottingham warned a leading Spiritualist that he was being 'misled to ruin by the enemy of God, the murderer of souls, and the liar from the beginning'. In 1917, the Vatican banned Catholics from attending séances, even as curious onlookers. Meanwhile, some mediums, overwhelmingly women,

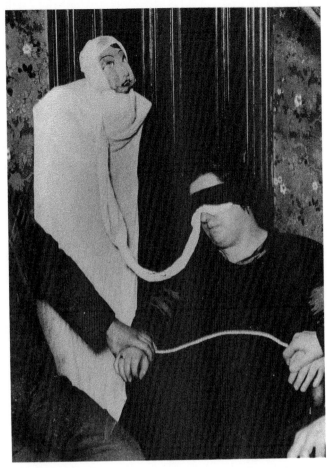

14. **Materialization medium Helen Duncan supposedly manifesting the spirit of a young woman, c. 1930**

were branded hysterics, and in America psychiatrists diagnosed 'mediomania' – insanity linked to Spiritualism.

The law also took a dim view. On both sides of the Atlantic, mediums were punished, in England under vagrancy or witchcraft legislation. A surge of Spiritualism after the First World War – the lost generation behind the veil – divided opinion. Many bereaved families derived comfort from séances, but government and police saw only exploitation. In 1944, Helen Duncan, a Scottish housewife, was successfully prosecuted for attempting to materialize spirits; the judge insisted that this was a case of fraud, but inevitably reporters wrote it up as a witch-trial. Duncan was the last person jailed under the Witchcraft Act, and the repeal was just a few years away. The emancipation of the Spiritualists did not, however, have the desired effect. The postwar world offered alternative forms of personal satisfaction: neo-paganism was one, television and consumerism were others. And freedom to worship exposed just how much the movement had thrived on prohibition. In 1961, the editor of *Psychic News* called the long-awaited change in the law 'the kiss of death'.

Chapter 8
Culture

Reinventing witches

In the summer of 1935, a team of German researchers began to scour the nation's archives, hunting for early modern witches. Overseeing the project was Reichsführer-SS Heinrich Himmler, to whom witches were either persecuted religionists of the Germanic race or magical warriors fighting demons – a 'black order' like the SS itself. Himmler hoped that the *Hexensonderkommando* would find millions of witches, but by the time work ceased in 1943, just 33,846 cases had been recorded. And what they revealed was that the witch's greatest enemies had been not clerical inquisitors but ordinary Germans.

The research, though flawed, has been useful to modern scholars. Himmler succeeded in bringing witches back to life, but because they were not what he expected their propaganda value was nil. The fact that our ancestors surprise us in this way is our fault not theirs. Many people claim to be haunted by the past, even that they see ghosts. But the dead don't bother us: we bother them – endlessly. Certain trades specialize in this: necromancers, sorcerers, Spiritualist mediums, and historians. Why? Because there is power in what precedes us; the dead are useful for understanding who we are in time.

Ghosts are symbols, conduits of encoded meaning; they are ambiguous, but that only increases their connectivity with our unconscious selves. As we saw at the beginning, witches, too, mediate between states of being: life/death, temporal/celestial, good/evil, desire/fulfilment – those opposites that we force apart but inwardly need to bridge to make sense of life. We all have a dark side, which Jung called 'the shadow self': a hidden, repressed version of ourselves at odds with our idealized public persona and societal norms. Only through the archetypes found in myths and folklore, Jung argued, can we discover who we really are, a process he called 'individuation'.

So witches are archetypes, stored inside individuals but originating in shared cultural sources and activated by similar experiences and emotions. Understandably, we want to hold them and their baleful history at arm's length while keeping an eye on both: it helps to know that others are more foolish and cruel than ourselves, be they witches or their persecutors. In April 2009, 1,000 Gambians charged with *maleficia*, including the murder of President Jammeh's own aunt, were set free thanks to the efforts of Amnesty International. In the previous year, a Nigerian crowd severely beat a woman they feared had transmuted from a cat – an echo of the Kent case from 1692. Good to be us, we say, not them. Yet the West has its own panics, scapegoats, rough justice, and torture chambers. When the witch-symbol bubbles up from our unconscious, it isn't always Ghoulish Gertie cackling on a broomstick: it might be a Muslim, a Jew, or a Roma. Archetypes know many stereotypes.

Meanwhile, the stereotype of the historic and folkloric witch has perpetual appeal, a visual package that entertains and frightens equally. Witches are everywhere: in books, dramas, pageants, and advertising; they inspire jokes, dreams, fables, similes, and metaphors. We never tire of reviving and reinventing them. Every 31 October, people turn their minds to witchcraft, especially the children decked out in black taffeta and green face-paint.

Halloween is rooted in Samhain, a Celtic festival marking the start of winter, a liminal moment of transition when the membrane between the living and the dead is most permeable. Whatever atavism is stirred in us when we gaze into a bonfire (or 'bone-fire', as it once was), today Halloween is light-hearted and commercialized. In the UK, it has displaced Guy Fawkes night (with its anti-Catholic roots), and in 2006 turned over £120 million, ten times what it had six years earlier. For some, Halloween is a time for remembrance as well as carnivalesque misrule. Modern covens and secular groups alike pay their respects to those who died in the witch-hunts.

Wherever you go, you find memories about witches. A Tuscan landowner once told me how in 1948 his mother had phoned the police to stop locals pushing an alleged witch into a communal oven. Thomas Robisheaux's book about Anna Schmieg began when he heard the legend while sight-seeing in Langenburg. The title of my own study of the medium Helen Duncan came from the owner of a guesthouse in Duncan's home town: 'Hellish Nell' was her childhood nickname. Stories are anchored in sites of memory. There are the dungeons in Colchester and Lancaster, where 17th-century witches once languished; and there is the Museum of Witchcraft in Boscastle, Cornwall, the relocated collection of Cecil Williamson and Gerald Gardner. You can visit the Witches' Cave of Zugarramurdi, centre of the 'Basque dream epidemic'. The town of Salem is a busy tourist centre replete with lurid attractions and New Age shops. By contrast, Salem Village (now Danvers), where it all began, is eerily quiet.

These places sate ghoulish appetites, but they also memorialize; usually, though, all we need is a simple stone or plaque and a moment to reflect. Witch-memorials have appeared in many places, from Scotland to Salem, part of a wider campaign to exonerate witches. Attainders on seven Salem witches were lifted in 2001, and in 2008 the Swiss canton of Glarus exonerated Anna Göldi, Europe's last executed witch (1782), on the grounds that she had been put through an 'illegal trial'. In Britain, a campaign to clear the name of Helen Duncan has been supported by the Salem Witch Museum and a Scottish baron, who himself has pardoned the 81 tenants from his estate burned as witches in the 16th and 17th centuries.

Witches always get attention, but should be handled carefully. Not all agree that historic witches should be pardoned: dissenting

15. Gerald Gardner (1884–1964), self-proclaimed father of modern paganism and wily manipulator of the history of witchcraft

voices in Glarus conceded that Anna Göldi's execution had been a 'misjudgement', but were 'not convinced that a rehabilitation in retrospect is possible'. Different times, different reality. We should also be wary of what we are told. In *Witchcraft Today*, Gerald Gardner claimed that Matthew Hopkins had tortured enemies of the puritan regime and 'picked up any unpopular old women on the way and had them executed'. The truth was otherwise. Gardner also owned a box of Hopkins's relics (authenticated by Margaret Murray), including a parchment talisman, a finger bone, and a crucifix-topped staff. It was a palpable hoax, as were Deacon's 'Tendring Witchcraft Revelations' (see Chapter 6), although this didn't stop them reappearing in a spurious 'biography of Matthew Hopkins' in 2006.

Dragging witches from past to present has other dangers. People get upset, like the Christian fundamentalists who destroy Harry Potter novels (see below), or the excitable pagan who shouted 'burn him!' at the end of one of my lectures in 2005. And when people get upset, they make mistakes. Feminist fury at the age-old oppression of women, much of it entirely justified, generated a literature dealing with witchcraft that amounted to little more than 'a twentieth-century horror fiction', to quote one historian. As Himmler found when he set up the *SS-Hexensonderkommando*, however darkly appealing, witches are less easily recruited to modern causes than they first appear.

Hogwarts and all

Today, the history of witchcraft is sophisticated. Embracing disciplines as diverse as psychology, iconography, and archaeology, academic writing is no longer triumphantly rationalist, nor soppily heroic or mock romantic, but bracingly *realistic*. The emic and the etic are balanced, and witch-beliefs understood from above and below and within. Thanks to both the 'new social history' of the 1980s and the 'new cultural history' of the 1990s, witchcraft is now seen as part of the early modern political and legal world, and a product of mentalities embracing popular religion and learned demonology. And a new generation of historians and literary scholars has used feminist theory to develop enormously subtle and penetrating analyses. (Diane Purkiss argues that 'the witch is not solely or simply the creation of patriarchy, but that women also invested heavily in the figure as a fantasy which allowed them to express and manage otherwise unspeakable fears and desires'.) University history departments run witchcraft courses tackling 'the reality problem'; students who avoid dodgy books and rubbish on the internet do well. But the fact remains that public memory of the witch-hunt continues to be rationalist and romantic: nurturing sublime, metaphysical aspects of witches' lives while censuring witch-hunters for their wickedness and ignorance. Fiction beats history.

Novels abound, from Harrison Ainsworth's *Lancashire Witches* to Gerald Gardner's *High Magic's Aid* (1949). I have a pile that relate to Matthew Hopkins alone; in one (comic) story, he becomes Ezekiel Oliphant, in another (for children) he is Obediah Wilson. In Julie Hearn's *The Merrybegot* (2005), he strays from eastern England and the period in which he lived. Witchfinders, like witches, are vulnerable to fictional manipulation. At the bottom of the heap is *The Witchfinders* by Ralph Comer (1968), where 'savage seventeenth-century practices of witch-hunting and burning still have an uncanny effect – 300 years later – on an entire village'; here a journalist gets drawn into 'the inhuman, primitive rituals of another age'. 1968 also saw Michael Reeves's cult movie *Witchfinder General*, starring Vincent Price, itself based on a trashy pot-boiler. The stark literality of film has a uniquely blurring effect on the boundary between fact and fantasy. Price *became* Hopkins, and the history of witch-hunting was rewritten for the general public. Also influential was the story of demonic possession at Loudun, fictionalized by Aldous Huxley in *The Devils of Loudun* (1952), and adapted as a play by John Whiting (1960) and a controversial film by Ken Russell (1971).

Best-known is Arthur Miller's dramatization of Salem, *The Crucible*, first performed in 1953. There have been two cinema versions, one in 1957 scripted by Jean-Paul Sartre, another in 1996 by Miller himself. To Miller, who was investigated for his 'un-American activities', Salem was an allegory for political paranoia: witches represented Communists, the judges Senator McCarthy and his ilk. Theatres, like courtrooms, are the natural home of witches, given the dramatic qualities with which onlookers invest them: malice, revenge, rebellion, remorse, pathos. Faust, the mythical scholar who swaps his soul for knowledge, has found many literary outlets, including Christopher Marlowe's tragedy *Doctor Faustus* (c. 1604), possibly a satire on John Dee. Jacobean audiences saw an increasing number of witchcraft plays, like Thomas Middleton's *The Witch* which drew on classical sorcery, continental demonology, and writing about English witch-trials such as Reginald Scot's book of 1584. Shakespeare read Scot to write *Macbeth*, which, like many 17th-century plays, exploited witches' innate theatricality but also their political associations; after all, *Macbeth* was written for James I.

But the perennial popularity of *Macbeth* lies not in politics or demonology but the universal appeal of a character who, like Faust, is destroyed by desire. Today, Faustianism is associated with the pact between man and modernism that has resulted in war, economic crisis, and ecological catastrophe. Meanwhile, witches populate theatrical genres apart from tragedy, from pantomimes to operas. Composers and librettists have found witches useful, everyone from Purcell, Mozart, and Wagner, to Harrison Birtwistle and Stephen Sondheim. Witches represent mystery and menace, especially the secret and seductive power of women over men. Gounod's *Faust* retains its vibrancy, and in 1961 composer Robert Ward adapted *The Crucible*. There have been musicals too, most iconically *The Wizard of Oz* (1939) and more recently its prequel *Wicked*, exploring the friendship between the future 'wicked witch of the west' and the 'good witch of the north'. At the time of writing, a Hollywood film of *Wicked* is in production.

Dozens of films have exploited witchcraft's possibilities, some comedies, many fantasies, but mostly horror movies. The earliest was *Häxen: Witchcraft Through the Ages* (1922), a documentary with lavish reconstructions. Its Danish director was inspired by the *Malleus Maleficarum*, and, like much early modern demonology, managed to be both high-minded and sensationalist, indulging the curious with images of depravity while warning of the dangers of superstition. The Hammer studios churned out spine-tingling entertainment for the postwar generation, establishing the core aesthetic for goth and heavy metal music mentioned in Chapter 2. No mystery, then, why Led Zeppelin guitarist Jimmy Page collected Aleister Crowley memorabilia, or one Midlands band called themselves 'Witchfinder General' (debut single: 'Burning a Sinner').

Like spooks, fairies, elves, pixies, and other beings that terrified our ancestors, in the Western world witches are mainly the cultural property of children. Kids in the 1960s and 1970s grew up with the winsome charms of *Bewitched*, in the 1990s it was *Sabrina the Teenage Witch*. There is no wickedness here, nor in the popular *Winnie the Witch* books. The most phenomenal success has been Harry Potter: J. K. Rowling's seven novels (and spin-off films, games, and merchandizing) about the boy-wizard and friends at Hogwarts School of Witchcraft and Wizardry. By June 2008, the books alone had sold over 400 million copies, in 67 languages. The brand is worth billions of dollars annually, although not everyone is so enthusiastic. In 2009, a former speechwriter to George W. Bush alleged that Rowling had been denied a presidential medal on the grounds that her books 'encouraged witchcraft'. Philip Pullman has also been vilified in America. Darker and more complex in its themes, Pullman's *His Dark Materials* trilogy (1995–2000) depicts good and evil witches doing battle in the skies. These witches are authentic Jungian archetypes: potent figures pricking our emotions, their origins in ancient history and mythology – a oneness with nature and culture.

The New Age

Sympathy with nature, and rejection of organized religion (another major theme in Pullman's novels) is a fundamental attraction of neo-pagan witchcraft. Today, the preferred term is 'Wicca', a religion involving ritual magic and observance of seasonal festivals. Wiccans are devoted to prehistoric deities, principally a male god manifested as a horned creature or as the sun, and a goddess in the form of a virgin-mother-crone trinity or the Graeco-Roman Selene, equivalent to the moon. As befits a liberal, intuitive faith, Wicca has different branches and traditions: Gardnerian, Alexandrian, Cochranian, Eclectic, Dianic, and so on. Wicca is increasingly polytheistic and personal, drawing on ancient paganism for modern usage, indeed in *reaction* to modern materialism. Compared to Christianity and Spiritualism, little emphasis is placed on animism and the afterlife; some Wiccans actively oppose the idea of pestering the dead.

Wiccans are misunderstood by a tabloid-reading public hungry for stories about sex and satanism. Relaxed morality and nudity do play a part in Wiccan beliefs and rites, although wearing robes is common. Montague Summers, Dennis Wheatley, and Hammer films have imprinted a picture of the sinister nocturnal ceremony where masked acolytes sacrifice a virgin, all pentagrams and black candles: the cover of Ralph Coman's novel shows hooded cultists leering at a naked girl on a black altar. The 1973 film *The Wicker Man* conjured this image vividly and memorably, enthralling millions, but doing no favours for the benign and compassionate neo-pagan movement.

At least Wicca is now recognized as a religion. The US military accepts Wicca as a valid faith, and in 2001 the Religious Identification Survey estimated that 134,000 Americans described themselves as Wiccans, compared to 8,000 a decade earlier. Worldwide, there may be as many as 800,000, although reliable statistics are elusive. Estimates of the number of practising witches

16. Publicity still from 1973 horror film *The Wicker Man*, in which pagan religion and poor harvests on a remote island lead to human sacrifice. Modern Wiccans do not endorse this sort of activity

in England vary between 3,000 and 30,000. Definitions are not always clear, though Wiccans insist they are a distinct denomination, separate from and predating the 'New Age'. Even so, there are plain and close affinities with the wider ethos of New Age spirituality, with its popular individualism, esotericism, naturism, and emancipation from dogma.

Wiccans still face implacable hostility from politicized Christian groups, especially in the United States. As campaigning Spiritualists discovered to their cost, a little opposition can be a good thing, uniting the group, sharpening their identity as freethinking dissidents from a redundant culture. Not all Wiccans claim ancestry (biological, spiritual, or cultural) from those executed for witchcraft in the 16th and 17th centuries, but most can identify with the idea of persecution for non-Christian faith. As Margaret Murray had intimated, witches are secretive because of prejudice, which then inevitably encourages fantasies about depraved rituals and sacrifices. The enemies of Wicca portray it as a deliberately or inadvertently satanic faith, an accusation vehemently denied by Wiccans, many of whom respect Christ and certainly have no truck with the Devil.

So we end as we began: with unstable terminology, myths, and stereotypes, clashing interpretations and ideologies – Samuel Butler's 'ungrippable shadow'. Witchcraft cannot be pinned down and labelled. It resists focus, and is endlessly reflected and distorted as in a hall of mirrors. Whether or not one believes in the existence of spirits and efficacy of magic, it's a fact that witchcraft exists. For millions of people, this is an unpleasant reality, far removed from the polite séance, seafront palmist, or Wiccan adoring the goddess. Vulnerable people are duped. In 2008, the UK's Fraudulent Mediums Act, legislation that had replaced the Witchcraft Act in 1951, was itself replaced by stricter consumer protection in reaction to the proliferation of mediums. As Christian churches lose their grip, and the world seems more dangerous, so spiritists and charlatans will meet the demand for reassurance. The Russian government is clamping down on witches (10,000 of them, according to a 2008 health ministry report) whose services include love spells and magical revenge, as if it were the 16th century not the 21st. One newspaper estimates the industry to be worth $30–$40 million per annum.

The reality of witchcraft gets much worse than that. Here are two stories from 2008. In February, a pregnant woman and her husband in Papua New Guinea were hanged by neighbours for malefic witchcraft. The woman gave birth as she struggled to free herself; parents and baby survived. Meanwhile, in Tanzania the authorities are fighting the trade in albino body parts for use in *muti* magic. 'People think we are lucky', said an albino member of parliament, 'that's why they're killing us; but we're not lucky'. In May, seventeen-year-old Vumilia Makoye was eating with her family when two men burst into their hut and cut off her legs; she died. The crisis has spread to Kenya, where in the same month as Makoye's murder, a woman had her eyes, tongue, and breasts gouged out. Tanzanian police link the craze to Nigerian horror movies which present witchcraft as a reality against which people should defend themselves with *muti*. The star of some of these is Helen Ukpabio, an evangelist who views the struggle with Satan in terrifyingly literal terms. In her *End of the Wicked* (1999), children's souls leave their bodies at night to attend a witches' meeting presided over by a white devil. Heinrich Kramer, Jean Bodin, or Pierre de Lancre would have understood exactly what was happening.

These cases impose limits on the relativism of the Western social scientist. Ukpabio's films encourage the persecution of Nigerian children, exemplified by the Child Rights and Rehabilitation Network which cares for them. In September 2009, a UN official identified witch-hunting as 'a form of persecution and violence that is spreading round the globe', affecting millions. We should sustain our disgust, and condemn the religious beliefs of the witch-hunters, however sincerely held. Equally, we shouldn't be complacent, defining ourselves against the people of Tanzania, Kenya, and Nigeria in a way that makes us feel intrinsically different. In addition to prejudice, real occult beliefs feature widely in the most developed societies on earth. German opinion polls between the 1970s and 1990s showed that between 10% and 20% of people believed in malefic witchcraft. The scale of belief in a personified Devil at work in the world, preying on sinners, is even more staggering. A Gallup survey in 1988 revealed that at least 50% of the citizens of economically advanced Catholic countries like Italy, Spain, and Ireland feared Satan; in the USA, it was 66%.

It's hard to imagine Salem happening again, but we would do well to remember that it might. After all, the 'reds-under-the-beds' scare of 1950s wasn't so different, as Arthur Miller appreciated; nor was the hysterical backlash after 9/11. Published photos of Satan's face in smoke from the Twin Towers, and girders on

Ground Zero twisted into a cross, played to real fears and beliefs – beliefs that make political mandates. Chances are you're lucky enough to live in an ordered society; but order is endangered whenever it is defended too zealously or unjustly. And reason is not enough to save us.

To be human is to feel emotion: to compete, loathe, destroy, and fantasize. We are good believers as well as good thinkers, mystics as well as scientists: the tendency is encoded into our DNA. In some, it's there on the surface; others need danger and desperation to bring it out. But we all fear the future, scorn opponents, and dream of success, and these are the basic ingredients of witchcraft. Perhaps in its essentials, then, the witch is just too useful a social archetype to be eradicated – a means to sublimate grief, expiate guilt, imagine desires, and project wrath. In your own mind, the line between good and evil may no longer be part of some apocalyptic struggle, dividing a morally reflexive universe of deities and demons, saints and sinners; but it does still exist, as Solzhenitsyn observed, drawn through every human heart.

References

Preface

Lucien Febvre, 'Witchcraft Nonsense or a Mental Revolution?', in Peter Burke (ed.), *A New Kind of History* (London, 1973), p. 185.

Chapter 1

The idea of witchcraft

Marina Warner, *Fantastic Metamorphoses, Other Worlds* (Oxford, 2002), p. 159.
Robin Briggs, *Witches and Neighbours* (London, 1996), p. 410.

Ancient wisdom

Bruce M. Hood, *SuperSense: Why We Believe in the Unbelievable* (London, 2009), pp. 46–55, 63–4, 96–105, 249–53.
Nicholas Humphrey, *Soul Searching* (London, 1995), ch. 8.

The rise of magic

Keith Thomas, 'Ways of Doing Cultural History', in Rik Sanders *et al.* (eds.), *Balans en Perspectief van de Nederlandse Cultuurgeschiedenis* (Amsterdam, 1971), pp. 77–8 ('emic' and 'etic').
Ludwig Wittgenstein, *Philosophical Investigations*, ed. G. E. M. Anscombe (Oxford, 1997), pp. 20, 47.
Shakespeare, *Macbeth*, act 4, sc.1, li. 48–9.

Chapter 2

Authority and orthodoxy

Tacitus, *The Annales and the Histories*, ed. Alfred John Church and
William Jackson Brodribb (Chicago, 1990), pp. 148–9.

Samuel Butler, *Notebooks*, ed. Geoffrey Keynes and Brian Hill (London,
1951), p. 193.

Thinking with demons

Butler, *Notebooks*, ed. Keynes and Hill, p. 62.

Augustine, *The City of God against the Pagans*, ed. R. W. Dyson
(Cambridge, 1998), pp. 359–89.

Canon Episcopi, in Henry Charles Lea, *Materials Toward a History
of Witchcraft*, 3 vols (Philadelphia, 1939), i, pp. 178–80.

Guillaume d'Auvergne quoted in Norman Cohn, *Europe's Inner
Demons* (London, 1993), p. 41.

Stuart Clark, *Thinking with Demons* (Oxford, 1997).

Secrecy and conspiracy

Errores Gazariorum (1437), in Alan Kors and Edward Peters (eds.),
Witchcraft in Europe, 400–1700 (Philadelphia, 2001), p. 160.

Kramer quoted in Christopher S. Mackay (ed.), *The Hammer of
Witches* (Cambridge, 2009), p. 120.

The National Archives (TNA), Assizes 45 10/3/34–54 (1673).

Jonathan Pearl in Richard Golden (ed.), *Encyclopedia of Witchcraft*,
4 vols (Santa Barbara, CA, 2006), iv, p. 988.

Margaret Murray, *The Witch-Cult in Western Europe* (Oxford, 1921).

Timothy D'Arch Smith quoted (about Summers) in Jonathan Barry
and Owen Davies (eds.), *Witchcraft Historiography* (Basingstoke,
2007), p. 77.

Montague Summers, *The History of Witchcraft and Demonology*
(London, 1926), pp. 110, 129.

Chapter 3

Healers and hags

Michael MacDonald, 'The Fearefull Estate of Francis Spira', *Journal of
British Studies*, 31 (1992), 61.

Cambridge University Library (CUL), EDR, B/2/5, 129–130, 213
(Mortlock, 1566).

Meurthe-et-Moselle archives, B9554 (Belz, 1580) – see http://www.history.ox.ac.uk/staff/robinbriggs/pdf/w331.pdf.

Canon Episcopi, pp. 178–9.

Kramer in Mackay (ed.), *Hammer of Witches*, p. 163.

Jeanne Favret-Saada, *Deadly Words* (Cambridge, 1990), p. 10.

Reginald Scot, *The Discoverie of Witchcraft* (London, 1584), pp. 7, 8.

The damage done

Mike Pitts, 'Urine to Navel Fluff: The First Complete Witch Bottle', *British Archaeology*, 107 (July 2009).

Richard Bovet, *Pandaemonium* (London, 1684), p. 87.

Valerie Flint et al., *Witchcraft and Magic in Europe: Ancient Greece and Rome* (London, 1999), pp. 54, 80–1.

E. E. Evans-Pritchard, *Witchcraft and Oracles among the Azande* (Oxford, 1976), p. 189.

J. D. Krige in Max Marwick (ed.), *Witchcraft and Sorcery* (London, 1982), pp. 268–9.

J. R. Crawford, *Witchcraft and Sorcery in Rhodesia* (Oxford, 1967), pp. 285–90.

Wolfgang Behringer, *Witches and Witch Hunts* (Cambridge, 2004), p. 224 (Cameroon sorcerers).

Patrick Leigh Fermor, *Words of Mercury* (London, 2004), p. 57.

A True and Exact Relation of the … Witches … in the County of Essex (London, 1645), pp. 20–1.

Hathorne quoted in Brian Levack (ed.), *The Witchcraft Sourcebook* (New York, 2004), p. 225.

Evans-Pritchard, *Witchcraft*, p. 25.

Ronald W. Clark, *Einstein* (London, 1973), p. 370.

Loathe thy neighbour

Keith Thomas in Mary Douglas (ed.), *Witchcraft Confessions and Accusations* (London, 1970).

William Monter quoted in Ronald Hutton, 'Anthropological and Historical Approaches to Witchcraft', *Historical Journal*, 47 (2004), 414.

Evans-Pritchard, *Witchcraft*, p. 5.

Robin Briggs, *The Witches of Lorraine* (Oxford, 2007).

Max Marwick, 'Witchcraft as a Social Strain-Gauge', *Australian Journal of Science*, 26 (1964).

Behringer, *Witches*, p. 25.

Evans-Pritchard, *Witchcraft*, p. 46.

Alan Macfarlane, *Witchcraft in Tudor and Stuart England* (London, 1970).

Keith Thomas, *Religion and the Decline of Magic* (London, 1971).

Peter Geschiere, *The Modernity of Witchcraft* (Charlottesville, VA, 1997).

Chapter 4

Debating Satan

Robert Boyle, *The Skeptical Chymist* (London, 1661).

Corinthians 11:14 (Satan as angel of light).

J. M. Keynes, 'Newton, the Man', in *Newton Tercentenary Celebrations* (Cambridge, 1947), p. 27.

How to find a witch

Lyndal Roper, 'Witchcraft and the Western Imagination', *Transactions of the Royal Historical Society*, 16 (2006), 141.

Alison Rowlands, *Witchcraft Narratives in Germany: Rothenburg 1561–1652* (Manchester, 2002), pp. 195–8.

Bishop Jewel quoted in James Sharpe, *Instruments of Darkness* (London, 1996), p. 89.

Charles Zika, *The Appearance of Witchcraft* (London, 2007), pp. 107–8.

Malcolm Gaskill, 'The Devil in the Shape of a Man', *Historical Research*, 71 (1998).

John Demos, 'John Godfrey and His Neighbours', *William and Mary Quarterly*, 33 (1976).

Evans-Pritchard, *Witchcraft*, pp. 31–2.

Brickbats and broomsticks

Wolfgang Behringer in Golden (ed.), *Encyclopedia*, iii, pp. 609–10.

George Mora (ed.), *Witches, Devils and Doctors in the Renaissance* (Binghamton, NY, 1991).

TNA, State Papers 16/271/15 (1634).

Thomas Jobe, 'The Devil in Restoration Science: The Glanvill-Webster Witchcraft Debate', *Isis*, 72 (1981).

Robert Latham and William Matthews (eds.), *The Diary of Samuel Pepys*, 11 vols (London, 1970–83), vii, p. 382; viii, p. 589.

Chapter 5

Custom and courts

TNA, PL 27/1–2.

Canterbury Cathedral Record Office, X.1.5, 162v, 163; X.1.2, 1/50; X.1.3, 156–8.

Norbert Schindler, *Rebellion, Community and Custom in Early Modern Germany* (Cambridge, 2002), p. 239.

John H. Langbein, *Prosecuting Crime in the Renaissance* (Cambridge, MA, 1974).

Christina Larner, 'Crimen Exceptum? The Crime of Witchcraft in Europe', in her *Witchcraft and Religion* (Oxford, 1984).

'Witch-craze'

Dan Brown, *The Da Vinci Code* (London, 2004), p. 173.

Michael D. Bailey, *Magic and Superstition in Europe* (Lanham, MD, 2007), p. 238.

Cohn, *Europe's Inner Demons*, pp. 181–5, 189.

Kors and Peters (eds.), *Witchcraft*, p. ix.

C. L'Estrange Ewen, *Witch-Hunting and Witch-Trials* (London, 1929).

Rowlands, *Witchcraft Narratives*, appendix.

Bengt Ankarloo and Gustav Henningsen (eds.), *Early Modern European Witchcraft* (Oxford, 1990).

Jonathan Barry *et al.* (eds.), *Witchcraft in Early Modern Europe* (Cambridge, 1996).

E. Le Roy Ladurie, *Jasmin's Witch* (Aldershot, 1987), p. 6.

CUL, Palmer B17, p. 20 (1465).

Brian Levack, *The Witch-Hunt in Early Modern Europe* (London, 2006), p. 182.

Perkins quoted in Stuart Clark, 'Inversion, Misrule and the Meaning of Witchcraft', *Past and Present*, 87 (1980), 119.

Pain and fire

Observer (8 March 2009), pp. 6–7.

Levack (ed.), *Sourcebook*, p. 215 (Malakurov).

Newes from Scotland (London, 1591), p. 28.

Wolfgang Behringer, *Witchcraft Persecutions in Bavaria* (Cambridge, 1997), p. 196.

TNA, STAC 8/140/23, m. 13 (1603).

Levack, *Witch-Hunt*, pp. 22–4, 93–4.

Behringer, *Witches*, pp. 149–51.

Chapter 6

Panic

Kors and Peters (eds.), *Witchcraft*, pp. 353–4.

De Valançay quoted in Briggs, *Witches and Neighbours*, p. 193.

A. L. Barstow, *Witchcraze* (London, 1995), chs 2–4.

Jenny Gibbons, 'Recent Developments in the Study of the Great European Witch-Hunt', *Pomegranate*, 5 (1998).

Richard Deacon, *Matthew Hopkins: Witch Finder General* (London, 1976).

Behringer, *Witches*, pp. 216–20.

G. L. Burr (ed.), *The Witch Persecutions* (Philadelphia, 1897), pp. 23–8.

Children

Michael MacDonald, *Mystical Bedlam* (Oxford, 1981), pp. 80–2.

CUL, EDR E44/3 (1646).

Centre for Kentish Studies, NR/JQp 1/30.

Lyndal Roper, 'Witchcraft and Fantasy in Early Modern Germany', *History Workshop Journal*, 32 (1991).

Barbara Ehrenreich and Deirdre English, *Witches, Midwives and Nurses* (Old Westbury, NY, 1973).

David Harley, 'Historians as Demonologists: The Myth of the Midwife-Witch', *Social History of Medicine*, 3 (1990).

TNA, Assizes 45 6/1/69 (1661).

Hans Sebald, *Witch-Children* (Amherst, MA, 1995).

Kors and Peters (eds.), *Witchcraft*, p. 354 (Würzburg).

Salem's lot

Levack (ed.), *Sourcebook*, p. 226 (Gray 1692).

Richard Slotkin and James K. Folsom (eds.), *So Dreadfull a Judgement* (Hanover, NH, 1978), p. 354.

John Demos, *The Enemy Within* (New York, 2008), pp. 189–212.

Cotton Mather, 'A Discourse on Witchcraft' (1689), in Kors and Peters (eds.), *Witchcraft*, p. 369.

Mary Beth Norton, *In the Devil's Snare* (New York, 2002).

Increase Mather quoted in Alan Heimert and Andrew Delbanco (eds.), *The Puritans in America* (Cambridge, MA, 1985), p. 338.

Sarah Rivett, 'Our Salem, Our Selves', *William and Mary Quarterly*, 65 (2008), 499.

Chapter 7

The reality problem

David Harley, 'Explaining Salem', *American Historical Review*, 101 (1996).

Joseph Glanvill, *Saducismus Triumphatus* (London, 1681), p. 8.

Brattle quoted in Heimert and Delbanco (eds.), *Puritans*, p. 339.

Francis Hutchinson, *An Historical Essay Concerning Witchcraft* (London, 1720), pp. 68, 167, 287.

Evans-Pritchard, *Witchcraft*, p. 32.

Emma Wilby, *Cunning Folk and Familiar Spirits* (Brighton, 2005), pp. 163–6, 189–90.

Experiencing witchcraft

Jeffrey Watt, *The Scourge of Demons* (Rochester, NY, 2009), p. 6.

Carl Jung, *Archetypes and the Collective Unconscious* (Princeton, 1981).

Sigmund Freud, 'A Seventeenth-Century Demonological Neurosis', in James Strachey *et al.* (eds.), *Complete Psychological Works*, 24 vols (London, 1953–74), xix.

Lyndal Roper, *Witch Craze* (New Haven, 2004), ch. 2.

Briggs, *Witches of Lorraine*, p. 117.

Edward Bever, *The Realities of Witchcraft and Magic in Early Modern Europe* (Basingstoke, 2008).

David Hall, 'Witchcraft and the Limits of Interpretation', *New England Quarterly*, 58 (1985), 273.

De Lancre quoted in Levack (ed.), *Sourcebook*, p. 107.

Sharpe, *Instruments*, p. 279 (Armstrong).

Magic redux

Athenian Mercury (28 February 1693).

H. H. Gerth and C. Wright Mills (eds.), *From Max Weber: Essays in Sociology* (New York, 1946), pp. 129–56.

Carlo Levi, *Christ Stopped at Eboli* (London, 1949), p. 13.

H. R. Trevor-Roper, *The European Witch-Craze* (London, 1969), p. 75.

Northampton Mercury (18 September 1752), p. 95.

Bishop of Nottingham quoted in Janet Oppenheim, *The Other World* (Cambridge, 1985), p. 84.

Simeon Edmunds, *Spiritualism: A Critical Survey* (London, 1966), p. 99.

Chapter 8

Reinventing witches

Walter Rummel in Golden (ed.), *Encyclopedia*, iii, pp. 806–8.

Daily Telegraph (19 March 2009).

Thomas Robisheaux, *The Last Witch of Langenburg* (New York, 2009).

Malcolm Gaskill, *Hellish Nell: Last of Britain's Witches* (London, 2001).

Independent (2 August 2007), p. 20 (Göldi).

Gerald Gardner, *Witchcraft Today* (London, 1954), p. 35.

Craig Cabell, *Witchfinder General* (Stroud, 2006) – 'spurious biography'.

Malcolm Gaskill, *Witchfinders* (London, 2005), p. 283.

Hogwarts and all

Diane Purkiss, *The Witch in History* (London, 1996), p. 2.

Nigel Williams, *Witchcraft* (London, 1987).

Celia Rees, *Witch Child* (London, 2000).

Ronald Bassett, *Witchfinder General* (London, 1966).

Alison Flood, 'J. K. Rowling Lost Out on US Medal over Harry Potter "Witchcraft"', guardian.co.uk (29 September 2009).

The New Age

Gazeta, Moscow AFP Agency (11 April 2008).

Reuters (23 September 2009).

Behringer, *Witches*, pp. 21–2.

Aleksandr Solzhenitsyn, *The Gulag Archipelago*, 2 vols (London, 1975), ii, p. 615.

Further reading

The literature of witchcraft is vast, although much is sensationalist, out of date, or otherwise unreliable. My purpose here is to identify some of the best writing, both to flag up recent ideas and to help readers discriminate. The focus remains historical: there are countless sociologies and anthropologies, novels and plays, which cannot be included. Even the list of good history is highly selective.

In writing this book I have relied on other syntheses, principally: Wolfgang Behringer, *Witches and Witch Hunts* (Cambridge, 2004); P. G. Maxwell-Stuart, *Witchcraft: A History* (Stroud, 2000); Michael Bailey, *Magic and Superstition in Europe* (Lanham, MD, 2007); John Demos, *The Enemy Within* (New York, 2008); Joseph Klaits, *Servants of Satan* (Bloomington, IN, 1985); Jeffrey Russell and Brooks Alexander, *A New History of Witchcraft* (London, 2007); and the *Athlone History of Witchcraft and Magic*, 6 vols (1999). For the early modern world, see: Brian Levack, *The Witch-Hunt in Early Modern Europe* (London, 2006); Robin Briggs, *Witches and Neighbours* (London, 1996). Richard Golden's *Encyclopedia of Witchcraft*, 4 vols (Santa Barbara, CA, 2006) is superb. See also the essays in Jonathan Barry *et al.* (eds.), *Witchcraft in Early Modern Europe* (Cambridge, 1996) and Stuart Clark (ed.), *Languages of Witchcraft* (Basingstoke, 1991).

England is covered by James Sharpe, *Instruments of Darkness* (London, 1996); Keith Thomas, *Religion and the Decline of Magic* (London, 1971); Alan Macfarlane, *Witchcraft in Tudor and Stuart England* (London, 1970); Malcolm Gaskill, *Crime and Mentalities in*

Early Modern England (Cambridge, 2000), chs 2–3. Useful older
works are: Wallace Notestein, *A History of Witchcraft in England from
1558 to 1718* (Washington, DC, 1911); C. L'Estrange Ewen, *Witchcraft
and Demonianism* (London, 1933); R. Trevor Davies, *Four Centuries
of Witch-Beliefs* (London, 1947). For Scotland: Christina Larner,
Enemies of God (London, 1981); Brian Levack, *Witch-Hunting in
Scotland* (New York, 2008); Julian Goodare (ed.), *The Scottish
Witch-Hunt in Context* (Manchester, 2002). See also: Patrick Byrne,
Witchcraft in Ireland (Cork, 1975) and Richard Suggett, *A History of
Witchcraft and Magic in Wales* (Stroud, 2008).

Works on specific European states include: William Monter,
Witchcraft in France and Switzerland (London, 1976); Robin Briggs,
The Witches of Lorraine (Oxford, 2007); Erik Midelfort, *Witch
Hunting in Southwestern Germany* (Stanford, CA, 1972); Wolfgang
Behringer, *Witchcraft Persecutions in Bavaria* (Cambridge, 1997);
Lyndal Roper, *Witch Craze* (New Haven, 2004); Marijke Gijswijt-
Hofstra and Willem Frijhoff (eds.), *Witchcraft in the Netherlands*
(Rotterdam, 1991); Julio Caro Baroja, *The World of the Witches*
(Chicago, 1965); Gustav Henningsen, *The Witches' Advocate: Basque
Witchcraft and the Spanish Inquisition* (Nevada, 1980); Carlo
Ginzburg, *The Night Battles* (Baltimore, 1983); Ruth Martin,
Witchcraft and the Inquisition in Venice (Oxford, 1989).

For the later period, see: Owen Davies and Willem de Blécourt (eds.),
Beyond the Witch-Trials (Manchester, 2004); Gustav Henningsen,
'Witch Persecution after the Era of the Witch Trials', *ARV:
Scandinavian Yearbook of Folklore*, 144 (1988); Ian Bostridge,
Witchcraft and its Transformations (Oxford, 1996); Owen Davies,
Witchcraft, Magic and Culture, 1736–1951 (Manchester, 1991);
Christine Worobec, *Possessed: Women, Witches and Demons in
Imperial Russia* (DeKalb, IL, 2001); Julian Goodare *et al.* (eds.),
Witchcraft and Belief in Early Modern Scotland (Basingstoke, 2008),
chs 9–10.

On Scandinavia and Eastern Europe, see: Bengt Ankarloo and Gustav
Henningsen (eds.), *Early Modern European Witchcraft* (Oxford,
1990); Per Sörlin, *'Wicked Arts': Witchcraft and Magic Trials in
Southern Sweden, 1635–1754* (Leiden, 1999); Gunnar Knutsen,
'Norwegian Witchcraft Trials', *Continuity and Change*, 18 (2003);
Gábor Klaniczay and Éva Pócs (eds.), *Witch-Beliefs and*

Witch-Hunting in Central and Eastern Europe (*Acta Ethnographica Hungarica*, 37, 1991–2); Michael Ostling, *The Devil and the Host: Imagining Witchcraft in Early Modern Poland* (OUP, forthcoming); W. F. Ryan, *The Bathhouse at Midnight: Magic in Russia* (University Park, PA, 1999).

Salem has its own bibliography. Start with Paul Boyer and Stephen Nissenbaum, *Salem Possessed* (Cambridge, MA, 1974); John Demos, *Entertaining Satan* (Oxford, 1982); Carol Karlsen, *The Devil in the Shape of a Woman* (London, 1987); Bernard Rosenthal, *Salem Story* (Cambridge, 1996); Mary Beth Norton, *In the Devil's Snare* (New York, 2002); Marion Gibson, *Witchcraft Myths in American Culture* (New York, 2007). Bernard Rosenthal's *Records of the Salem Witch-Hunt* (Cambridge, 2009) assembles all the documentary evidence in one massive volume.

For other primary sources, see: Alan Kors and Edward Peters (eds.), *Witchcraft in Europe* (Philadelphia, 2001); Brian Levack (ed.), *The Witchcraft Sourcebook* (New York, 2004). For classic essays: Brian Levack (ed.), *New Perspectives on Witchcraft, Magic and Demonology*, 6 vols (New York, 2001); Darren Oldridge (ed.), *The Witchcraft Reader* (London, 2002). On historiography: Jonathan Barry and Owen Davies (eds.), *Witchcraft Historiography* (Basingstoke, 2007); Diane Purkiss, *The Witch in History* (London, 1996); Wolfgang Behringer, 'Historiography', in Golden (ed.), *Encyclopedia*, ii, pp. 492–8; Malcolm Gaskill, 'The Pursuit of Reality', *Historical Journal*, 51 (2008).

Key anthropology (other than Evans-Pritchard) includes: Max Marwick (ed.), *Witchcraft and Sorcery* (London, 1982); Mary Douglas (ed.), *Witchcraft Confessions and Accusations* (London, 1970); G. L. Chavunduka, *Witches, Witchcraft and the Law in Zimbabwe* (Harare, 1982); Ray Abrahams (ed.), *Witchcraft in Contemporary Tanzania* (Cambridge, 1994); Peter Geschiere, *The Modernity of Witchcraft* (Charlottesville, VA, 1997); Isak Niehaus, *Witchcraft, Power and Politics . . . in the South African Lowveld* (London, 2001); Sohalia Kapur, *Witchcraft in Western India* (Hyderabad, 1983); Jeanne Favret-Saada, *Deadly Words* (Cambridge, 1990). See also Ronald Hutton, 'Anthropological and Historical Approaches to Witchcraft', *Historical Journal*, 47 (2004).

On witchcraft pre-1500, see: Matthew Dickie, *Magic and Magicians in the Greco-Roman World* (London, 2003); Daniel Ogden, *Night's Black Agents* (London, 2008); John Gager (ed.), *Curse Tablets and Binding Spells* (Oxford, 1999); Eugene D. Dukes, *Magic and Witchcraft in the Dark Ages* (Lanham, MD, 1996); Richard Kieckhefer, *European Witch Trials … 1300–1500* (London, 1976). For the heretical roots of witch-hunting, see: Gary Waite, *Heresy, Magic and Witchcraft in Early Modern Europe* (Basingstoke, 2003); Michael Bailey, *Battling Demons* (University Park, PA, 2003).

For more on the idea and imagery of witchcraft, see: Stuart Clark, *Thinking with Demons* (Oxford, 1997); Gerhild Scholz Williams, *Defining Dominion* (Ann Arbor, MI, 1995). For popular communication: Marion Gibson, *Reading Witchcraft* (London, 1999); Robert Walinski-Kiehl, 'Pamphlets, Propaganda and Witch-Hunting in Germany', *Reformation*, 6 (2002); Charles Zika, *Exorcising Our Demons* (Leiden, 2003). On gender, see: Willem de Blécourt, 'The Making of the Female Witch', *Gender and History*, 12 (2000); Merry Wiesner-Hanks, *Women and Gender in Early Modern Europe* (Cambridge, 2008), ch. 7; Robin Briggs, 'Women as Victims?', *French History*, 5 (1991); Deborah Willis, *Malevolent Nurture* (London, 1995); Lara Apps and Andrew Gow, *Male Witches in Early Modern Europe* (Manchester, 2003); Jonathan B. Durrant, *Witchcraft, Gender and Society in Early Modern Germany* (Leiden, 2007).

Popular magic is described well in Owen Davies, *Cunning Folk* (London, 2003); Emma Wilby, *Cunning Folk and Familiar Spirits* (Brighton, 2005); Wolfgang Behringer, *Shaman of Oberstdorf* (Charlottesville, VA, 1998); and Richard Godbeer, *The Devil's Dominion* (Cambridge, 1992). On demonic possession: Nancy Caciola, *Discerning Spirits: Divine and Demonic Possession in the Middle Ages* (Ithaca, NY, 2003); Sarah Ferber, *Demonic Possession and Exorcism in Early Modern France* (London, 2003); James Sharpe, *The Bewitching of Anne Gunter* (London, 1999); Marion Gibson, *Possession, Puritanism and Print* (London, 2006).

Finally, the modern age. On Spiritualism, see: Alex Owen, *The Darkened Room* (Cambridge, 1989); Janet Oppenheim, *The Other World* (Cambridge, 1984); Molly McGarry, *Ghosts of Futures Past* (Berkeley, CA, 2008); Jenny Hazelgrove, *Spiritualism and British Society between the Wars* (Manchester, 2000); Malcolm Gaskill,

Hellish Nell (London, 2001). For occultism: Alex Owen, *The Place of Enchantment* (Chicago, 2004); Ronald Hutton, *The Triumph of the Moon* (Oxford, 1999); T. M. Luhrmann, *Persuasions of the Witch's Craft* (Cambridge, MA, 1989); Helen Berger, *A Community of Witches* (Columbia, 1999); Margot Adler, *Drawing Down the Moon* (New York, 1986).

Index

Witchcraft